THE STAY-AT-HOME ENTREPRENEUR

THE
STAY-AT-HOME
ENTREPRENEUR

125 Ways to
Earn Money While Raising
Your Family

JAY DAVID

AVON BOOKS ◆ NEW YORK

AVON BOOKS, INC.
1350 Avenue of the Americas
New York, New York 10019

First Avon Books Trade Paperback Printing: April 1999

AVON TRADEMARK REG. U.S. PAT. OFF. AND IN OTHER COUNTRIES, MARCA REGISTRADA, HECHO
EN U.S.A.

Printed in the U.S.A.

OPM   10   9   8   7   6   5   4   3   2   1

We are most grateful to Paul Baldwin for his creative efforts in helping us put this book together.

CONTENTS

The Writing Game

The Animal Kingdom

And How About . . . ?

FIVE
Home Business Success Stories   158

INTRODUCTION

Would you like to earn some extra money? Most people would. Would you like to earn some extra money without having to leave the house, working for yourself while raising a family? Hundreds of thousands of Americans are doing just that in small towns and big cities in every corner of the United States. If you would like to join that throng of people, generating both cash and personal satisfaction, this book will tell you how to go about it.

The first three chapters will explain how to find the time to start your own small business even if you are already busy with your children, and suggest ways to find the space in your home to conduct your new venture. You'll learn the basic principles of conducting a home business and the best ways to promote your service or product for the least amount of money. Chapter Four, the core of the book, lists 125 different ways that people are already making good money with home businesses; some you will no doubt be familiar with, others are unusual and remarkably creative. Each of the 125 possibilities is explored in some detail to give you a sense of how such a business could work for you. Many of these possible choices of home business opportunities may surprise you, and you're likely to find at least a few that will make you say, "I could do that." That's exactly what thousands of people now running home businesses thought when they read an article in a magazine or heard about someone in town who's making money selling things they make or offering a wide variety of personalized services. We all have talents we've never fully explored, abilities we could put to use in new ways. *The Stay-at-Home Entrepreneur* is designed to help you discover those talents in yourself and put them to good use.

The book closes with a selection of success stories—and there are many others you will read about throughout the earlier chapters. This is the book to inspire you to become one of those success stories yourself.

THE
STAY-AT-HOME
ENTREPRENEUR

ONE

Finding Time and Space for a Home Business

Time is the most valuable thing a person can spend.
THEOPHRASTUS, THIRD CENTURY B.C.

Remember that time is money.
BENJAMIN FRANKLIN, 1748

To make extra money at home, you must spend the time to earn it. If you have three toddlers underfoot at home, finding that extra time can be difficult. It can be done, of course. If you can give even half an hour a day to a task like making Christmas ornaments for sale, you can finish enough over the first two thirds of the year to make a tidy sum during the Christmas season. The best-selling novelist Danielle Steele wrote her first novel, *Passion's Promise*, in the early morning hours, before her large family was awake. And if you run errands a lot but have an ability to concentrate no matter where you are, a great deal can be accomplished at ballet classes and in doctors' waiting rooms.

It's all a matter of time management. This is one of those corporate phrases that intimidate some people. But you have in fact been managing time ever since you were old enough to think for yourself. You managed to get your homework done, didn't you? You were able to work things out so you could be on the basketball team and be in the school play. Your summer job as a teenager didn't keep you from seeing all the new movie hits and still doing the chores expected of you at home. And in managing your home, you have undoubtedly met deadlines, juggled several projects at once, and met crises head-on.

You already know a lot about managing time. Still, some people are better at it than others, and even thinking about finding the time to undertake a home-based job gives many people pause. Some people say, "I'll never stick to it without having a boss looking over my shoulder." Or "Well, I can't get fired, so I'll be lazy about it." The answer to that kind of feeling is to reverse the thoughts. Say to yourself, "How nice it will be not to have a boss looking over my shoulder." Or "Since I can't get fired, I'll be able to relax and enjoy the work more."

Your stay-at-home job should be something you like doing a great deal. It may be something you already do for pleasure and have simply never thought about doing to bring in money. At this point you may not be sure what you might like to do as an at-home job—one of the main purposes of this book is, of course, to help you find out how to use talents or skills that you may not fully recognize as potential moneymakers. But your at-home job should be one that gives you pleasure. If it's going to be sheer drudgery, you're probably better off taking a part-time job outside your home.

But even though your at-home way of making money is something you enjoy doing, it will require organization and self-discipline. These words are listed in that order because good organization helps to create self-discipline.

A Working Space

The first step in getting organized is to decide where you are going to work. Sometimes this is self-evident. If you are going to grow herbs for sale or give gardening lessons, the space you work in will primarily be your garden. If you've decided to do a job that involves carpentry, you probably already have a shop set up in your garage or basement or tool shed. But there are many pursuits that could be done at several different locations in your home. If you're going to be writing articles, or a book, it can be done at the kitchen table if you prefer writing a first draft in longhand, as a surprising number of writers do. But the kitchen table can be a bad place to work if you have a tendency to snack or have children running around. Then you'll be better off setting up a desk—or even a card table—someplace where you can close the door. Your bedroom perhaps, or that little room in the back of the house that is basically a junk room now. And if you are going to do your writing on a personal computer, you will need more space to accommodate the printer and perhaps a copier as well. It could be important to have a space big enough to have a number of reference books close at hand. It would be absurd to have your writing space in one room and have to go off to another one to check the dictionary or look up a needed fact. Talk about wasting time.

If you are making crafts or doing artistic work, you're going to need a space big enough to keep your supplies in, which may include not only paints but tools, Styrofoam forms, ribbons, beads, and any number of other basic materials. They should all be right at hand, on shelves or in labeled boxes so that you don't have to lose time looking for what you need. The cellar, attic, or garage may provide the space you need if you can't set aside a whole room for your work.

If you are involved in cooking to earn extra cash, your center of activity is obviously going to be the kitchen. But you will need to reorganize your cabinets so that you can put everything you need for your extra-money cooking in spaces devoted to that purpose. There may be some pots and pans or knives or kitchen tools that you will use for cooking family meals as well as the food product you are selling. But all ingredients that go into whatever you are selling should be kept completely separate—that not only saves time but facilitates good bookkeeping. There should also be a separate cabinet for canning jars, platters, or any other containers or serving dishes you are using in your business. If you jumble what you use in your private life together with what you use in your business, you are going to end up wasting time down the line figuring out your expenses.

Once you've got your work space set up, make it clear to your family that the space belongs to you and nobody else. If you've set up a home office space, the supplies located there are for your business and nothing else. Make clear that you won't tolerate your spouse or your kids jumbling things around looking for rubber bands or a red pen or notebook paper. If you have an at-home food business and your teenage kids tend to raid the kitchen, put locks on the cabinets with your working supplies in them. Put locks on anything you can if it proves necessary.

Your working space should be yours, but if you have to use the kitchen or dining room table, clear away what you've been using when you've finished working and put it in a designated space that other people in the house know they mustn't touch. Using a communal space like the kitchen table to work at obviously will put a kink in your management of time, but sometimes it can't be avoided. Just be sure to include the setup and put-away time in your schedule.

Scheduling Your Work

Procrastination is the thief of time.
EDWARD YOUNG, 1745

Some people—not many—do not schedule their work time at home. There are people with the ability to work at home on a very flexible basis, doing nothing one evening and putting in four hours the next. But they are unusual, and unless you know from past experience that you can get a great deal accomplished that way, it is vital to make a working schedule and stick to it. Most people who do not schedule their work time end up procrastinating, which the Webster's Unabridged Dictionary defines as "to postpone or defer taking action." It is all too easy to procrastinate yourself into a panic, and have to stay up half the night to meet a deadline, or worse, miss it altogether. The great majority of at-home jobs have deadlines that must be met. If you haven't got the party dress ready on time, or the television set repaired when you said it would be, your business is going to go the way of any other business, large or small, that misses deadlines: down the drain. At-home work depends greatly on word-of-mouth advertising, and if you don't have work finished as promised, you will lose out in a big way. Word of mouth can be negative as well as positive, and if you mess up, you can lose a lot of customers in a hurry.

Scheduling means blocking out specific work times and following them. It does not mean trying to do a great deal of work in a very short period of time. That's overscheduling. Overscheduling can be almost as bad as no schedule at all. Ironically, it's the people who work the hardest who tend to get into trouble here. There's a myth that every expert on time management warns about: the belief that people work best when they are under pressure and that trying to do too much at once will create a beneficial time crunch. People who believe this myth are confusing time pressures with what's known as "rising to the occasion." Sure, there are athletes who play their very best in Super Bowls and actors who give extraordinary performances on opening night. But that's the pressure of *occasion*, not time—and you will have noticed that there are athletes and actors who seem to be at their worst in Super Bowls and on opening nights, which is why they lose and get bad reviews.

"Crisis management" is what gets even huge corporations into trouble. Don't schedule your at-home work so that you create crises for yourself. It's far better to overestimate the amount of time a task will take than to underestimate it. Especially when you are first starting out in your chosen at-home vocation, give yourself *too much* time to get things done. If you have time left over, you can start a new project or take a well-deserved break.

As you become more experienced, you will be able to

tighten up on the amount of time you give yourself to do a task. But start out slowly. It's hard for people in our frenetic age to realize it, but there are a lot of things that get done better at a slower pace. And just because you associate that concept with advice on sex from Dr. Ruth doesn't mean it is without application in other spheres! There's a word for work that's done in too much of a hurry. The word is *shoddy*.

How much time should you spend on your at-home job? The answer to that lies in individual circumstances. Since you have kids, you are inevitably going to have less time to devote to your at-home work than a single person or a married person without children. But it is generally wise to set aside units of time that will make it possible to complete something, whether it's a whole process or a step in the process. That may mean only half an hour if you are making small craft items for sale.

Take those Christmas ornaments previously mentioned. Certain kinds of ornaments may take only half an hour each to complete from start to finish. With others, you may be able to finish off the first step—a basic coat of gold paint, say—on half a dozen objects. Next work session, you could do the second step, and so on. In fact, any project that requires letting paint dry properly is best approached in this kind of step-by-step manner.

Many other kinds of work, from refinishing furniture to repairing machinery, are longer-term projects, and it is sometimes difficult to be certain how long a given part of the process will take. In these cases, schedule enough time—an hour, two hours—to make it possible to complete at least one step, even if that only means taking apart a piece of machinery to see where the problem lies.

If you get a step done more quickly than you expected, and it's clear that you have time to complete an additional step, fine, go ahead and do it. But if the time you have allotted is going to expire shortly, knock off for the day. It's always best to stop when you have completed a full step in your working process. Psychologically, it's a boost to know that a step has been finished.

If you stop in the middle of a step, on the other hand, you have less of a sense of accomplishment and may even find yourself confused about where you were when you take up the job again. Of course, if your lifestyle makes it possible to engage in open-ended at-home work sessions, that's terrific. But even in that case, it's better to stop at an obvious break-off point.

For some projects, it's necessary to work all the way through from start to finish. This is likely to be true if you are preparing food for sale. But cooking is one of the easiest things to schedule since recipes always have built-in cooking times. Even with cooking, however, it is sometimes possible to divide the work into two sessions. If you're making appetizers for a cocktail party, for example, much of the basic preparation can probably be done one evening, with the finishing touches put on the next day.

Weekdays, Weekends, or Both?

The preceding example, about preparing appetizers for a cocktail party, brings up a new question. Is your at-home work going to be something you do only on weekends, or can it be scheduled on weeknights as well? Cocktail parties usually begin between five and six o'clock in the evening. If you are your children's only caregiver during the week, you may not be able to put the finishing touches on the hors d'oeuvres and have them ready to be picked up, or have time to deliver them, on a weekday. This would have to be a weekends-only job. You could take care of a party on Saturday, and another on Sunday, or even more than one on each day, but you won't be able to do it for a Wednesday. Other kinds of cooking, of course, like making jams and jellies or putting up bottles of herbed vinegar or infused oils, can be done after the kids have gone to sleep.

But even if your at-home work could be done on weeknights, is that the way you want to organize your time? This is entirely a matter of personal preference, although the more time you spend doing your at-home job, the more money you're likely to earn. Some people want to make *some* extra money, but don't want to push themselves *too* hard, and prefer to limit their at-home work to weekends. Others may lead fairly social lives, or spend more time with family on the weekends, such as going to kids' sporting events, and get their at-home job done on weeknights. There are particularly industrious people who will work at home on both weeknights and weekends.

But be careful not to overextend yourself, especially at the beginning. Yes, there are workaholics who can keep going for endless hours. But even Bill Gates, who in the early years of Microsoft used to work two days straight and then go to sleep under his desk, reached a point in his late thirties when he admitted that he needed a good seven hours sleep a night to be at his best. There have been a number of recent studies and articles about the fact that Americans in general suffer from sleep deprivation. Too little sleep is bad for one's physical and mental health. Government studies have shown that many more on-the-job accidents occur among those who aren't getting enough sleep. If you don't get enough sleep, or exhaust yourself by working too many hours, both your family life and your at-home work will suffer in the long run.

Many people find that the best way to schedule at-home work is to do some work two or three nights a week, and put in somewhat longer hours on weekends. Those who seem happiest about their at-home work see to it that they still get time to relax or play. In fact, the most common use to which the extra money earned at home is put is vacation trips, although many other uses, from clothes to electronics to college funds for the kids, are also prevalent.

How you decide to schedule your at-home work is an individual decision based upon both the kind of work you are doing and the shape of your life in general. But do make a schedule and do your best to keep to it. Inevitably there will be times when you can't adhere to that schedule. You or one of your children may be ill, or relatives may come to town, or some unexpected occasion may disrupt your usual at-home working hours. But that can happen with any kind of plan or schedule. Having a plan and a schedule remains important in and of itself.

Keeping Distractions at Bay

Life is not so short but that there is always time
for courtesy.
RALPH WALDO EMERSON, 1876

Ralph Waldo Emerson was long regarded as the most American of philosophers. But there are those who now see him as somewhat old-fashioned. He lived in a more leisurely age, people will say, and while courtesy is all very well, something to be practiced when possible, our fast-paced, bottom-line age requires toughness above all.

That may be true in the corporate world, and the kind of good manners that emphasize courtesy seem to be on the wane all around us.

But if you are going to operate a small, at-home business in your spare time to make extra money, courtesy is *extremely* important. Many at-home businesses are service-oriented. Whether you are giving beauty treatments or repairing antique clocks, you are not going to build a customer base unless you take the time—sometimes extra time—to be courteous. People don't expect much courtesy in shopping malls, but they do expect it from people who run small businesses. Indeed, that's one reason why they go to independent, one-person operations in the first place—to get the kind of personal attention that they have difficulty finding elsewhere.

Yet there is a problem that at-home workers often run into that sometimes makes rudeness seem like a good idea. It's not a problem involving the at-home worker's customers but rather the worker's friends and family. Many people who get into at-home work discover that at the beginning there is a tendency on the part of family and friends not to take that work as seriously as they ought to. It's not that they're going to disparage what you are doing; on the contrary, they are likely to think it's terrific that you're using your talents this way. But despite their apparent enthusiasm, they may feel that because you are working at home, on your own time, it is perfectly okay to *interrupt* your work any time they feel like it.

Your family is likely to prove easier to deal with than your friends in this regard. You can be franker with your family, and flat out lay down the law with your kids. To your family you can say, "My at-home work time is my time, and don't interrupt me unless it's an emergency. If there's something you need to talk about with me, do it before I start working, or wait until I'm through."

In fact, you may even be able to get your older kids involved in what you're doing, and enlist their help. That depends on the kind of work you're doing, of course. You can't have the kids around while you give someone a facial or when you're processing tax returns. But sometimes there are preliminary or organizing steps that kids can help with. And you can certainly ask them to pitch in if you are stuffing envelopes with advertising flyers to promote your at-home business.

But friends, especially at the beginning, can be a real problem. They may call you up "just to find out how you're doing with your new effort." The answer you might like to give is, "Well, I was doing fine until you interrupted me." That's not courteous, but neither is their telephone call. Some people won't see it that way, of course. They will think they are being great friends, and very solicitous, by calling to see how you're doing, and if you tell them off, they're going to be angry. (The same goes for your mother or mother-in-law, who will call to see "how things are going," when they are really testing your seriousness or sending a message that you ought to be paying attention to your children or your spouse.)

There's an answer to this problem. It's called an answering machine. If you don't have one already, get one. And if you're working in a part of the house away from the answering machine you have, install a second one where you work. Get the kind that allows you to hear the voice of the person calling, so that if it is a client or customer you're expecting to hear from, you can pick up the phone if necessary. Put a message on the answering machine that makes it very clear why you're not picking up. In your cheeriest voice, record a message that says, "I'm hard at work right now, but I'll get back to you as soon as I can." Instruct other members of your household that if they pick up the phone in another part of the house, to say you're working right now, but they'll see that you get the message.

Not only should you have an answering machine, you should let friends and relatives know your working schedule. Tell them very specifically that you've decided to work from seven-thirty to nine-thirty on Tuesday and Thursday evenings. That information, together with your answering machine message, will soon get across the fact that you really are not available to chat during those hours. In our contemporary world, answering machines are accepted—if only barely in some quarters—as a substitute for old-fashioned courtesy.

Getting Down to Work

Little strokes,
Fell great oaks.
BENJAMIN FRANKLIN, 1750

You've made a space in your home in which to work. You've found the time in your busy life to get the work done. The next two chapters will help you to deal with the business aspects of your at-home job, from bookkeeping to advertising. But having committed the time and found the best working space you can manage, you have already taken the two most important fundamental steps toward a successful at-home endeavor that can bring in extra money. Even if the time you have been able to allot to start with is limited, and the space less ample than you could wish, you are on your way.

As you begin your new endeavor, though, be patient. Carving out the time to do your work is one thing, but now another aspect of time comes into play. Nothing happens overnight. Some people who start an at-home extra job get lucky and have surprising success right from the beginning. But for most people, it takes a while to get fully established, to build a customer base, as your advertising and the all-important word-of-mouth recommendations of your first satisfied clients spread the news that you do very good work.

Don't get discouraged if sales or customers are slow in the early going. You're starting something new, and only time can bring the rewards you're looking for. Remind yourself that with time, as Benjamin Franklin put it, even little strokes can fell great oaks. And also keep in mind another old saying about oak trees, this one anonymous but with us since Roman times: "Mighty oaks from little acorns grow." A great many people have had such great eventual success with an at-home business that it has grown to be a full-time one, in some cases even a business with a national customer base instead of a local one. Not everyone who starts an at-home business even wants that kind of supersuccess, of course. But it's still nice to know that such an outcome is in the realm of possibility.

TWO

Running a Home Business

*Government proposes, bureaucracy disposes. And
the bureaucracy must dispose of government
proposals by dumping them on us.*
P. J. O'ROURKE, 1991

Regulations! There are regulations about practically everything in modern society, and starting a small at-home business is unfortunately no exception to that fact. But if you get yourself properly organized up front, and then put aside a modest amount of time at regular intervals to make certain that your business records are up-to-date, this aspect of working at home does not have to be onerous.

Just don't put yourself in the position of having to use the "I didn't know I was supposed to do that" excuse.

You should know what you are supposed to do, and this chapter will give you the basic facts about the rules, regulations, and procedures you need to be aware of. But since state and local laws can vary widely, some of the considerations raised here may apply to you while others do not.

Local Business Licenses

The word *local* means the county and/or municipality in which you live. Even within the same state, different counties can have varying laws on the books, depending on whether they are largely urban, suburban, or rural, and even on what political party is dominant in the area. Similarly, a small town and a large city in the same county may have quite different regulations. Generally speaking, the greater the population of a given community, the more rules and regulations there are. But local governments can be very quirky. There may be new laws on the books that you aren't fully aware of, and there may be laws going back a hundred years that don't make much sense in the modern world and are seldom enforced. But *seldom* is a very important word. If someone decides he or she doesn't like what you're doing, and there's a law on the books that applies in any way, no matter how antiquated the law is or how long it has been ignored, it can be invoked and can cause you trouble.

That means that you must check carefully to see what laws might affect the business you want to start. The time to do this is right at the beginning, as soon as you start seriously considering the possibility of developing an at-home business. Even if you haven't fully made up your mind to go ahead, find out what the local licensing laws are. What you discover may in fact be crucial in helping you to decide whether to proceed. Above all, don't spend a dime on anything else until you've checked out the laws that may apply to your prospective business. Don't buy any supplies or invest in any machinery until you know what the local regulations are.

Some home businesses are particularly likely to require some kind of license or permit: those that affect public safety or public health. For example, anything that involves preparing food for sale, whether you are catering cocktail parties, baking pies on weekends, or putting up fancy jams and jellies, is likely to require not only a license but also health inspections. There are some rural areas where selling pies on the front lawn is a tradition and there are no licenses required. But don't go by appearances. Just because there's a lady two miles away who has a jelly stand in front of her house and she tells you she doesn't have a license doesn't mean one isn't required—her son may be on the police force and so her lack of a permit is "overlooked." Because food production is so strictly regulated, you need not only to check with city hall about a permit, but also see to it that the board of health sends an inspector around before you sell so much as a single pie. Many people who have gone into some sort of food business have found that it was necessary to remodel their kitchens, or even set up a separate kitchen, in order to comply with regulations.

You want to open a beauty parlor in your home, or hold aerobics classes? You're almost certain to need a permit of some kind, as a matter of public safety. You're thinking of starting an obedience school for dogs or a "beauty service" for pets? That's likely to be a matter of both public health and public safety. Day care, whether for toddlers or the elderly, is likely to require a license, as is opening a bed-and-breakfast.

Well, you may think, all I'm going to be doing is writing speeches for professional people on my PC; surely I'm "home free." Don't bet on it. The labor laws in several states require that *all* commercial activities conducted at home be licensed. In others, of course, only a few will require a commercial permit, usually doctors, lawyers, and accountants. But once again, these laws can be quirky, and they can also be suddenly changed. In the summer of 1997 the City of Los Angeles passed a new law requiring all writers working at home to get a license. The Screen Writers Guild, a major power in Hollywood, immediately filed suit to have the law thrown out as a constitutional violation of First Amendment rights to free speech. But we live in a time when communities are looking for any way they can to raise a few more bucks for the city treasury, and the trend everywhere is to require more licenses, not less.

So phone city hall, or go there yourself, and find out what kind of license or permit you are going to need, if any, and how much it is going to cost. Fees are usually modest, although they can run to several hundred dollars for some business activities in some areas. If the fee seems out of line in terms of the budget you were developing for yourself, you can shelve your idea or come up with another one that doesn't require as high a fee or any at all. But if, after reading this section, you have any thought of trying to go ahead without checking on licenses and permits, hoping to "get away with it," DON'T DO IT! The fines for breaking a licensing law can bankrupt people—and have.

Zoning Laws

Checking on local zoning laws is just as important as finding out about licenses and permits, and should be done at the same time. If you live in a locality of any size, that will probably mean dealing with an entirely different governmental office, but the failure to do so can not only get your business closed down but can cost you heavy fines, quite possibly involving criminal charges. Don't be naive about this. You can ask your neighbors on both sides if it's okay with them if you start a home business. But getting their approval does not mean you're square with the city government. Remember that grouch in the next block who won't even respond to a friendly hello? That's just the person who will be on the phone to the police the minute he or she becomes aware you're in business. If you have all the proper papers and are in accordance with zoning laws, such complaints will have no force, but woe betide you if you're not in accordance with the law.

Zoning laws can be out-of-date, even absurd. Times change and neighborhoods change. Many communities are trying to update their zoning laws so that they will make sense for the large numbers of people who "telecommute," working full-time for a company but using a computer link that allows them to do their jobs at home three or more days a week. If you come up against a zoning law that seems ridiculous, contact the office of your local elected representative to the city council or county board and find out if there's any prospect of the law being changed in the near future.

Sometimes zoning problems can be overcome by getting a variance. This may just be a matter of filing papers, and a routine variance will be granted after a short time. But it can also mean appearing at a hearing at which your neighbors are given the opportunity to vote yes or no on the variance. A public announcement of your variance request will be made in advance. Most people can't be bothered to go to zoning board meetings, but that can mean that the meddlers and naysayers will be overrepresented. Talk to any neighbors with whom you are particularly friendly, and if they think what you want to do is just fine, urge them to show up at the meeting and vote in your favor.

What's in a Name?

You need to have a name for your business even before you deal with licenses and zoning permits, because that name will have to go on any forms you fill out. Choosing a name for a business is a curious process, and can have odd results. We associate the name Tiffany with very high priced luxury goods, particularly jewelry, and the name Woolworth with inexpensive dime-store goods—including low-level costume jewelry. But when those utterly different businesses were started in the nineteenth century, each simply made use of a family name.

In fact, the great majority of American businesses, from the most famous to the least known, use family names. Kellogg's cereals, Campbell's soups, Ford cards—family names all. Of course, that doesn't always bring success. The automobile named for Edsel Ford turned into one of the great jokes of American commerce. Nor does a strange, even unattractive, name spell disaster. Think of Smucker's jams, which in recent years capitalized on that somewhat off-putting name with its ad line "With a name like Smucker's, it's got to be good."

But there are some cases in which it is unwise or even illegal to use a family name. A name that's difficult to pronounce can bring problems because everyone will say it differently, leading to a lack of focused recognition.

Take the name Campbell. If you are going to be selling a food product, you'd better not use it. It doesn't matter that your own name is Campbell. As a national food brand, it can't be used again by anyone making food. If you try, you'll get sued. And don't think that because you live off the beaten track, nobody will find out. You never know when a second cousin of the man in charge of the Campbell's advertising account will drive through town!

You can't use copyrighted characters, either. "Goofy's Dog Care" is a name that will get you a stern letter from the Disney lawyers—the company even sued the Academy Awards for using Snow White in an opening number without permission back in 1989. And don't think you can get away with being cute. Selling a food product called a McNibble will just bring on the McDonald's lawyers.

Some names don't fit well with the product being sold. "Ida's Homemade Pies" sounds great, but "Tiffany's Home-Baked Pies" doesn't quite cut it. First names, if they have the right ring to them, are very good choices for homespun foods or crafts, however. And if you're doing any kind of repairs or reconstruction, first names can also help get across the idea that you're easy to talk to. Joe's or Ed's (or even Sally's) Engine Tune-Ups sounds just fine.

But many people are tempted to give their small at-home businesses more imaginative or elevated names. Just don't get carried away. Too fancy a name, when attached to a small business, will just cause people to giggle.

You will also have to make sure that the name you've chosen hasn't already been taken by some other business in your area. Every city government keeps a fictitious-name file, a listing that is formally called a "DBA" (doing business as). If the name you've been considering is listed, you can't use it. You will also have to file your own form, to protect yourself, and renew it about every five years. Even so, unexpected problems can crop up.

There is a famous story about a very popular New York City restaurant that opened across from the new Lincoln Center for the Performing Arts in the late 1960s. It was owned by the actor Patrick O'Neal and his brother. They decided to call it "O'Neal's Saloon," and had already installed a large, expensive neon sign when they were informed by the city that it was illegal to call anything a saloon—a law that went back to Prohibition. The O'Neals took the easy way out, changing *Saloon* to *Baloon*, even though that meant that *Baloon*, which should have a double *l*, was misspelled. The restaurant went on to be a great success, but there is a lesson here. Don't have signs made, or print business cards or advertising, until you are certain the name you've chosen is free and clear.

Banking and Accounting

Every expert in the home business field recommends the opening of a special bank account solely for your business. Even if your home business cash flow is going to be modest at the beginning, having a separate bank account for it brings numerous dividends. It makes it much easier to keep account books, since there will be no need to go through after the fact and separate out personal checks and deposits from business ones. Your business account gives you more credibility with customers and suppliers, and will make your bank take you more seriously if you later wish to apply for a business loan for expansion or other purposes. A business account also has a beneficial psychological effect, enhancing your own sense of yourself as an entrepreneur. And for those who have a tendency to be lazy about accounting, it acts as a reminder, even a goad, to keep accurate books and update them regularly.

Before opening a business bank account, it is wise to apply for a *federal employee identification number*, referred to as an EIN. Technically, you do not have to do this unless you are going to hire people to work for you. In that situation *your* EIN and *their* Social Security number must both go on the tax forms you file for them. But even if you are the sole proprietor of your business, with no employees of any kind, having an EIN will make your bank look on you with greater regard, and can be important in getting trade discounts for supplies or machinery.

Your business bank account can serve as a strong underpinning for your accounting procedures. Paying for materials and supplies by check as much as possible will help to keep track of your disbursements. Ask your bank about getting an ATM/check card. This is a recent development in the banking industry, but is becoming more and more common. These cards are NOT credit cards, even though they are emblazoned with the logo of one of the major credit card companies. They allow you not only to withdraw cash from an ATM machine, but—more to the point for the small business person—to draw directly on your bank account to pay for any purchases made at a store or dealership that accepts Visa, for example, or to pay by check if the store does not have electronic access equipment.

Since an electronic disbursal directly from your bank account means that the money has been "withdrawn" that instant, you must keep close track of such transactions, just as you would with an ATM withdrawal. You will, of course, be provided with a receipt on the spot, but it is vital to record the transaction in your records as soon as possible. It should be noted that ATM/check cards originally had inadequate protections against their use if they were stolen, unless the bank was immediately notified of their loss, but under pressure from consumer groups and bank regulators, that situation is rapidly being rectified.

That brings us to developing an accounting system for yourself. If you have a personal computer, and are adept at using it, you will probably want to invest in spreadsheet software that will allow you to keep your accounts on your computer. However, be sure you get software that is flexible and not more complicated than your business requires. Spreadsheets can be extremely important to larger companies, but there are even experts in the computer field who think they are more complicated than most people really need.

If you do not have a personal computer, or, having taken a look at a friend's spreadsheet setup, think that it is a more difficult and complex way of keeping books than you need or can handle, there is nothing wrong with doing it the old-fashioned way. Any office store offers a variety of accounting books. Take your time to look them over and choose the one best suited to your requirements. Then USE it. Some people like to put incoming checks into one basket, and receipts for outgoing expenses in another, and tote them up once or twice a week. This is a perfectly valid way of keeping accounts, but it is probably better to set aside a few minutes at the beginning or end of each scheduled work session to bring your books up-to-date. People who do not have personal computers usually make use of a small pocket or desk calculator to do mathematical calculations. And there are still people, good at arithmetic, who feel more secure using pencil (or pen) and paper—they like to see that column of figures fully displayed. But whatever method you use, update your books regularly and often.

Keeping proper accounts of expenditures for the raw materials needed for a business can be more difficult in some areas of work than others. One of the most complicated kinds of expenditure to keep track of is the purchase of food when you are in the catering business or even making pies. The problem here is that it saves time to do the food shopping for yourself and your family simultaneously with making purchases for your business. But if you have everything on one cash-register slip, you will have to go over it line by line later, separating out and recording all your business expenditures. You have to have such information not only to keep track of how much money your business is making but also for tax purposes. You also must keep all such register receipts, and if you are ever audited by the IRS, the agent is not going to look kindly on receipts that intermingle personal and business expenses, even if you have carefully put a check mark beside each business expenditure. The best way to avoid confusion is to keep personal and business items separate in the shopping cart, and ask to pay for each group independently so that you get separate register slips. It's even better if you can take a child or spouse along with you and use two different shopping carts.

This is just one example of the complications that can ensue from having a home business. *You must always keep the expenditures for the two separate.* It's a problem that can arise in a surprising number of home businesses, from gardening enterprises to sewing.

If you are one of those people who are truly terrible at keeping accounts, it is probably best to get someone else to do them for you. Some home business entrepreneurs are able to call on a spouse or a friend to do the accounting for them, but it is better to pay an outsider than to end up with chaotic accounts. If you do need to hire a professional, ask for recommendations from friends, co-workers, or, best of all, other people with small, independent business ventures. The individual you hire does not necessarily have to be a C.P.A.—it could even be someone who, like you, has a side business at home. In fact, such a person would have a particular understanding of your situation. Stay away from the yellow pages on this one—a lot of the people you find listed there will not have much experience with home businesses.

Accounting is a chore for most people. But it is an essential aspect of running a home business, and it does have side benefits. It will give you a very clear picture of how you are doing, and can force you to think more carefully about how to cut costs or whether it might be time for you to raise your prices a little. You will be able to judge precisely how effective a new advertisement has been, leading you to do more like it or to seek other ways to make your wares or services known. And there is nothing more cheering than going over your accounts and seeing how your business has grown, even little by little, as the months go by.

Good accounting is also the key to effective budgeting. Anyone going into a home business needs to draw up a budget before getting started, of course. You need to estimate the costs of materials and equipment and decide on the prices you will charge on the basis of these costs, so that you make a reasonable profit. What that profit would be is difficult to pinpoint. Some home businesses can bring in a very large return for minimal investment if the practitioner is particularly talented.

For example, a person who paints portraits may be able to realize quite large profits relative to the cost of materials and the time invested. But this is also a riskier business than some. If the artist is good enough to command three hundred dollars for a portrait, the number of people who can afford to pay that much may be limited, even though those who do have the money to spend think the result is well worth it. On the other hand, the profit margin on home-baked pies will be much smaller, but it can also be a steadier business. Before anyone starts a home business, he or she should be comfortable with the estimated profit. If the potential profit doesn't seem worth it, then there's no point in starting the business.

But the budget for almost any home business should change as time goes on. Your accounts will tell you how you are doing, and point the way to saving money here or investing additional money there to increase your business and your profit. Indeed, if you have a great success and come up with the equivalent of a Cabbage Patch Doll or a game like Trivial Pursuit, which turned into huge national fads, your initial budget and your early accounts may come to look decidedly quaint.

Taxes

Some people are whizzes at doing their own taxes. If you're one of them, you don't need any advice. If you're not one of them, you need a tax accountant. Yes, that will cost money. But having one will take a great deal of worry out of running a home business, will go a long way toward keeping the IRS out of your hair, and will prove invaluable if you do have the bad luck to get audited. And getting audited does have a lot to do with luck.

At present—and this could change, anything can change when it comes to the IRS—audits are being conducted at random on a revolving list of professions, and that lottery can land anyone with a booby prize. Forms also get audited if they trigger alarm bells on the IRS computers—one of the most important reasons for having your taxes done by a professional is to avoid triggering those alarm bells.

Selecting a tax accountant is one of the most important decisions you will make. Don't go to one of those storefronts that open up in January and close down at the end of April. You want someone whom you consult at any time of the year if necessary. Also keep in mind that there are many different kinds of tax accountants, with many different specialties. You want someone who has a number of other clients who own home businesses. Larger cities will have tax experts who specialize in freelancers of various kinds, writers, artists, actors, and they can also be a good bet for the home business owner. In smaller communities, ask around. Seek out other people who have home businesses, whether part- or full-time, and get their recommendations.

The tax laws in recent years have changed to make it much more difficult to deduct home-office expenses and to reduce the deductions that can be taken for entertainment expenses. Much bigger changes may be coming. The growth of the computerized information highway, the increasing number of people who are working at home, and many other factors are going to have marked effects on tax laws. There is also a growing political constituency backing a flat tax and the abolishment of the IRS.

Some of the big changes are years away, but tax law is in a very fluid period, and smaller changes that affect home businesses may occur at any moment. Even as things stand, a part-time home business can mean filing a slew of additional tax forms, including those for self-employment (Social Security) taxes, profit and loss forms, and filing tax information for anyone you may employ to assist you in your new enterprise. Save every receipt from your expenditures and copies of every bill you charge your clients or customers, and get some expert advice. It will be worth every penny.

Lawyers

Lawyers are expensive. And because they are, there is a large and growing body of do-it-yourself books on the law, covering everything from wills to incorporating. What's more, the wrong lawyer can cause you more trouble than no lawyer. One of New York's foremost literary agents once told me that whenever a celebrity came to him about writing a book, and insisted that his or her lawyer be party to the deal, the agent stayed out of the situation, no matter how potentially lucrative. That's because, he said, most lawyers haven't got a clue how publishing works, but that doesn't keep them from putting their noses in and messing things up.

There are, of course, literary lawyers who specialize in publishing. But this story emphasizes the fact that most lawyers are specialists, and even those who are generalists may have little knowledge about many kinds of problems.

Small at-home businesses are a growing feature of American life, but there are still many lawyers—top-notch people in other areas—who know practically nothing about them. So if you think you need a lawyer, take your time asking around, talking with other home business entrepreneurs, to find one who has experience with at-home business problems. If you already have a personal lawyer, by all means approach him or her about your new needs. But don't be shy about asking point-blank about how much experience your lawyer has had with at-home businesses. If he or she has had very little, you need to go to someone else. And if your lawyer gets mad about that, then maybe you need a new one altogether.

If you think you're up to trying to deal with some low-level legal situations on your own, go to the library or a major bookstore and take a look at what's available. There are many books on matters that a home business person might encounter, and many include sample forms that are legal in all, or almost all, states. (The exceptions will be noted.)

A recent book, updated in 1997, that has been recommended by many entrepreneurial magazines is the *Legal Guide for Starting & Running a Small Business, Volume I*, by Attorney Fred S. Steingold, published by Nolo Press. Take a look at this or other books in the field, and if you still feel at sea, consult a lawyer.

Incorporating Your Business

Incorporating is a fad these days. Even freelancers such as musicians and writers sometimes do it. There's no question that it creates instant status. But it is also expensive. It can cost as much as fifteen hundred dollars to create a corporation, and one thousand dollars per year to maintain it because of the annual fees involved. There are two types of corporations, denoted by the letters C and S. Unless you are interested in having a board of directors and shareholders for your homemade bread business, a C is not for you.

An S corporation is the more usual route for a small business. Because it establishes a business entity that is separate from the person who owns it, it creates a legal buffer if disaster strikes, whether a personal injury suit or bankruptcy. Someone teaching aerobics classes, where the possibility of physical injury exists, or someone who is canning food, where the possibility of food poisoning exists, might want to consider incorporation for that reason alone. An S corporation is less expensive than a C corporation to form and maintain, but it could still cost more than additional insurance.

One of the supposed advantages of incorporation is a saving on taxes. At least that's what you'll hear at cocktail parties. Listen to an expert, Daniel Sitarz, author of *Incorporating Your Business,* published by Nova Publishing Company: "Depending on many factors, the use of a corporation can increase or decrease the actual income tax paid in operating a corporate business."

Incorporation may indeed be something you want to consider if your business becomes such a roaring success that you are turning it into a full-time job and hiring a number of employees to do the additional work. Let's hope you have such a success, but short of that, you are probably going to be just as well off with what the IRS terms a "sole proprietor" business. That means that you control it, all profits go to you, and your income from the business is taxed at the personal level. You are personally responsible for your business under this arrangement, but you can't be fired from it, like Apple Computer founder Steve Jobs was, by a board of directors.

Speaking of computers and incorporating, Bill Gates did not turn Microsoft into a corporation until five years after he and Paul Allen founded the company, even though they were already doing millions of dollars of business.

Insurance

As suggested in the preceding section, even many at-home businesses are going to need extra insurance. If you have anyone coming into your home in connection with your business, even if you're just giving voice lessons, consult with your insurance agent about extending your personal liability insurance to cover your new situation. No matter what kind of home business you run, in fact, it would be wise to consult your insurance agent. That doesn't mean letting yourself be scared into exorbitant and unnecessary insurance. But look into the matter, consult with friends and family as well as any other at-home businessperson you know, and think it over. You've launched on an exciting new journey. It's certainly a time for optimism. But new ventures also mean new responsibilities—that should be part of the excitement. You're taking charge of your life in a new way. And taking charge means paying attention to the issues raised in this chapter, so that you can forge ahead feeling entirely comfortable about the adventure you've embarked upon.

THREE

Promoting Your Home Business

The codfish lays ten thousand eggs,
The homely hen lays one.
The codfish never cackles
To tell you what she's done.
As so we scorn the codfish,
While the humble hen we prize,
Which only goes to show you
That it pays to advertise.
ANONYMOUS, EARLY TWENTIETH CENTURY

Every time we buy a car, a soft drink, or a box of cereal, part of the price we pay goes toward the astronomical sums spent by major corporations to advertise their products. For the individual starting up a small at-home business to bring in some extra cash, the mere mention of the millions of dollars it costs for a sixty-second spot on a

Super Bowl broadcast can be intimidating. The beginning entrepreneur can get a queasy feeling wondering how many hundreds of dollars it will cost to do even small-scale local advertising.

You certainly are going to have to advertise, but it is possible to start out on a very small scale and increase your advertising budget gradually as your customer base increases. Because you won't have the overhead involved in renting a store location, you can make some money even with a modest customer base at the start.

What's more, on a local level the most important aspect of promoting your business can be good word of mouth. That's not only free advertising, but the best kind you can have. You're going to have to spend some money on advertising, too, and this chapter will discuss how to get the most for your money through a number of different advertising forums. But you can get a start by creating word-of-mouth interest before you spend a penny on more conventional forms of advertising.

When you are ready to start your at-home business, telephone all your friends and any local relatives. Tell them what you are doing. If you are offering a service, whether it's giving voice lessons or doing taxes, talk about why you've chosen this line of work and give your credentials. But you can go beyond that if you are making crafts, baking cheesecakes, or knitting baby sweaters.

Showing people what you can make, or in the case of food, having them taste it, can create a considerable buzz. Take one of those cheesecakes to a PTA meeting and pass out samples at coffee break. Bring in some of the decorated eggs you're selling and show them around. If you're painting portraits, put a couple of examples up on your wall before friends come over. You may get some sales right off the bat, but even if you don't, you will get people talking and create an awareness of what you are doing.

Are you making dolls? Give one to your best friend's daughter for her birthday—the other little girls at her birthday party may want one, too. Are you making Christmas ornaments or any other kind of small craft items? Give some to friends and neighbors as Christmas presents. The same goes for jars of homemade jelly, fancy herb vinegars, or other gourmet treats you are making.

If you are starting a catering sideline of any sort, give a party to showcase your talents. Many of your close friends will already know about your skill in the kitchen. (Some have probably even said, "You should start a restaurant with food this delicious.") This party isn't for them, though. Your guest list for a demonstration party should be made up of people who don't know about your abilities. Don't hesitate to invite people you know only slightly. Send out invitations that make clear that it's a promotional party, but that there's nothing to buy, just lots of delicious food. Few people can resist free food. Do you know anybody, no matter how casually, who's a reporter or an editor at the local paper? Be sure to invite him or her. It could lead to an eventual human interest story in the paper about your sideline business.

And if you're making food items or crafts, watch for any upcoming neighborhood street fair or church fair where tables are set up with things for sale. Even if the proceeds go to the neighborhood association or the church restoration fund, this can be a good investment. Contact the fair organizers to reserve a place. Be sure to have business cards on hand, and don't just have them displayed in a little box—hand one to each customer. When the proceeds of such a sale are being donated, this effort can cost you as much as a fair-sized newspaper ad, but because seeing—or tasting—is believing, it can be equally effective as a means of making your talents known, and go further toward creating good word of mouth. What's more, local newspapers often cover church and neighborhood fairs, which could lead to a mention of your wares in a small news item.

Newspaper Ads

There's no question, however, that newspaper ads are going to be important to your business. Some people like to start out with an ad several square inches in size in the appropriate news section. That generally means the Home or Style section for crafts, food, furniture refinishing, sewing, beauty, or other products and services related to personal or home enhancement. Tax preparation, word-processing services, and the like should appear in the business section, while services such as car or lawnmower repair would belong in an automotive section.

But an ad of any size, especially if you want to feature a photo or use any fancy typefaces, can cost quite a lot, and many home-based workers find that this kind of ad is more effective after the business is established. A great many home-based workers, in fact, start out with an inexpensive three- to six-line ad in the advertising section at the back that includes the Help Wanted ads. Here you will find entries devoted to items for sale and various services, as well as a listing of announcements, usually at the beginning of the section.

The Announcements section is something of a catch-all, but is often glanced at by casual readers out of curiosity. This can be a good place to have your ad if you are offering an unusual service such as "word doctoring," which involves editing and rewriting speeches, reports, or other written documents. Most newspapers are very good about advising local advertisers about which section to place an ad in—after all, if the ad works successfully for you, you will be back to place additional ones.

Many newspaper readers pay more attention to the ad pages at the back than you may realize. Even so, it is usually wise to run your ad for several days in succession or a full week. The longer the ad is to run, the cheaper the rate per day. In smaller cities or larger towns that have a daily paper, you should be able to run an ad for a week for well under one hundred dollars. If you live in a very small town or rural area where there is only a once-weekly paper, you will spend much less and benefit from the fact that most people read every word. Many suburban areas are covered by a newspaper from the nearest large city, which can mean the ad will be more expensive, but such locales often have a weekly paper that focuses on a smaller area, and that may be the better choice, both in terms of expense and because most at-home businesses can't expect, at least at the start, to draw customers or clients who live more than a few miles away.

Communities all over the country often have another kind of newspaper as well—one that contains little or no actual news but is simply an advertising circular of fifteen to twenty pages that is distributed free at supermarkets and other stores. These publications are a real boon to the at-home business. The advertising rates are very cheap, and because it's a free circular, a great many people pick one up out of habit every week.

The effectiveness of even small, back-of-the-paper ads in the local newspaper, or in a weekly circular, can be considerable. But how you word your advertisement can make a big difference in the kind of response you get.

There are some basic rules here. First, make crystal-clear what you are selling or the kind of service you are offering. If you find you've taken three full sentences to describe what you're offering, you need to start over. In ads, clarity almost always means brevity. Second, *do* use adjectives to attract attention: "*adorable* dolls," "*expert* repairs," "*delicious* party platters," "*professional* word processing," "*gorgeous* wreaths." But remember that one well-chosen adjective will do a better job than three fuzzy ones. "Adorable, huggable, lovable dolls" is overkill—any one of those three words by itself will get a clearer message across.

But you may want to emphasize other aspects of your work, as well. Then it's fine to use an additional adjective of a different kind, as in "adorable *handmade* dolls." But often it's best to break things up, as in "professional word processing. Fast, accurate." The words *fast* and *accurate* are qualities associated with professional work, and give added emphasis. But if you say, "fast, accurate, professional," you lose the impact of the additional words. Similarly, "delicious, beautiful party platters" isn't as effective as "delicious party platters, beautifully presented." Yes, that's adding another word, *presented,* that you'll be paying to have in the ad, but it gives a much more elegant tone—and the idea of elegance is just what you want to get across.

What should your ad say about the prices you charge? This can be tricky. But there is one absolute rule: NEVER use the word *cheap*. The word *cheap* has all kinds of unfortunate associations, from "shoddy" to "cheapskate." The word *inexpensive* is better, but not really good enough. It will draw calls from bargain hunters, but they often turn out to be such "cheapskates" that even your low prices won't be good enough for them. There are many better words or phrases to use. "Excellent value," "affordably priced," and similar phrases work well if you're trying to keep the cost of your ad down. But sometimes it is worthwhile to use a few more words. For example, you could say, "Adorable dolls, handmade quality at machine-made prices." That suggests that you're offering a superior product at the same price a customer would pay at the mall for a more commonplace gift.

Of course, in many cases you should give a specific price. If you're offering a word-processing service, find out what the going rate is in your area, and then undercut the competition slightly. Any item or service that there's a common standard for in your area can be specifically priced at a competitive rate. Some at-home businesses can involve giving a range of prices. If you prepare appetizers for cocktail parties, for example, you could say, "Menus range from $3 to $12 per person." Not only does a range of prices give a variety of customers the feeling that you might have what they are looking for in terms of price, but it also subtly suggests a high level of competence on your part, since you are able to adjust to different kinds of needs.

With these guidelines in mind, take your local paper and study the ads in it carefully. Circle ones that you think are particularly good in red; put a blue circle around the ones you think are pretty bad. Compare the good ones with the bad ones, and figure out what the differences between them are. Then make a draft of your own ad. Ask family members and friends what they think of it. Revise your ad according to any suggestions they have that you think are valid. But don't make any changes that go against your own instincts. Feedback from others can be helpful, but some suggestions are also better ignored.

You can often phone in an ad and pay for it by credit

card. But if it's not too inconvenient, it can be worthwhile to go to the offices of the paper. The people at the ad desk—which is often in the lobby—can be very helpful and make good suggestions about how to pare down your ad by a couple of words. They may also have ideas about which section your ad will be most effective in. It's often wise to run a new ad for only a week, and see what kind of response you get. If it is disappointing, that may be a sign that your ad needs to be rewritten, somehow refocused.

As time goes by, you'll find that you become more adept at composing ads. What you've learned will be helpful when you take the bigger step of placing a larger ad in the body of the newspaper, along with the news stories. Much of what you learn can also be applied to ads in other mediums—flyers, direct-mail ads, radio and television—although each medium will require some adjustments.

Flyers

Once your business is fully established, you will want to start thinking about additional ways to advertise beyond generating word of mouth and through the local newspaper. For the majority of at-home businesses, the logical next step is flyers. Flyers can be a single sheet, printed on one side only, or they can be more elaborate. Let's start with the single-sheet flyer.

The single-sheet flyer is usually the size of a standard piece of typewriter paper, 8½ by 11 inches. This makes it easy to run off on a copy machine, and it can be folded like a letter and stuffed into a standard business envelope, or simply folded in three like a business letter, secured with a gummed sticker to keep it closed, and mailed out that way, with the reverse side of the top fold giving you an empty space on which to write an address.

There's no point in producing a flyer unless it's going to look professional. It shouldn't be done in handwritten script unless you have a gift for calligraphy. Some people have made calligraphy their at-home profession, turning out beautiful wedding invitations, baby announcements, and formal place cards for sit-down dinners. Obviously such an individual would want to show off his or her talents in a flyer. But calligraphy can be striking in a flyer advertising any craft item. You wouldn't want to use it to advertise small-appliance repair or clerical services, though—it would seem at odds with the kind of work you do.

Most flyers use typographical lettering. If you have a personal computer, you can use the available print styles to put together a handsome piece of work. There are special software applications that can give you a multitude of choices. But don't get carried away. People sometimes are so excited by the possibilities afforded by their PC that they produce flyers in which every line is printed in a different typeface. This ends up looking messy and confusing. Two, or at most three, different typefaces are much more effective. Be sure that in using different typefaces, each one is reserved for a particular kind of information. For example, you might use one for the attention-grabbing headline, another for the body of the ad, and a third for information on how to contact you.

If you don't have a PC yourself, perhaps you have a friend who would be willing to format your prepared flyer ad on theirs. Or you can take your ad to a printing shop and have them help you choose typefaces as well as print the flyer for you. But that is a more expensive route.

Copy machines are so good these days that you can easily do the job yourself, even in color, once you have the master sheet for the ad put together. Color is great, of course, always an eye-catcher. But unless you are including a photograph of your craft or artwork on the flyer, it may not be worth the extra expenditure.

Once you have your flyers printed, there are several ways to distribute them, which you can use singly or in combination. The cheapest way to get them seen is to put them on bulletin boards. Keep an eye out for public bulletin boards at schools, churches, even businesses. In smaller communities, merchants you often do business with may be willing to tape a flyer to the inside of their front window. Sometimes flyers show up nailed to telephone poles, but be careful about this since many communities have laws against "defacing" telephone poles, or allow such displays only for yard sales, with strict requirements about removing the ad afterward.

You could also distribute your flyer by simply walking around your neighborhood and pushing folded flyers through mail slots. If you have kids, here's an opportunity for them to help you out; they may even be able to persuade some school friends to distribute flyers in their own neighborhoods. Flyers can also be mailed, of course, either folded and sealed with a gummed tape (the post office doesn't allow the use of staples for this anymore) or stuffed in business envelopes (another job for your kids). That takes us to the use of direct-mail advertising.

Direct Mail

Direct mail is used by a large number of companies, both on the national and local levels. But keep in mind that other phrase used to describe direct mail—"junk mail"—and think carefully about using this form of advertising before investing in large amounts of postage. It's only a small loss if the flyer you hand-delivered by walking around your neighborhood goes directly into the waste-basket. But if you've paid postage on it, you could be throwing away a lot of money.

Consider how likely it is that a flyer received in the mail is going to net you a new customer or client who hasn't responded to your newspaper ads. Does the volume of your business—the number you can produce, or the number of beauty appointments you have time to schedule—really warrant a direct-mail approach to advertising? National advertisers are happy if a direct mailing brings a response from even 10 percent of the addresses to which the mailing went. Is that kind of return worth the expenditure to you?

In addition, exactly who are you going to send your ad to? Large companies have computer bases to draw on, information they have built up over many years or have paid another company to provide. Some people in at-home businesses have friends with access to mailing lists, but they may not be ones that have any real application to your own business. Of course, you can spend some time going through your local telephone book and sending out flyers at random. Sometimes this can work, but it is mostly a matter of luck when it does.

This is not to say that you shouldn't even consider direct-mail advertising. It has paid off for some at-home businesses. One woman spent many hours driving around the ritziest section of town with a friend who wrote down the names on mailboxes. These were then checked out in the telephone book. The woman then prepared a direct-mail ad and sent it out. She had a very good response, because she was able to target a specific kind of potential customer for her business, which was a gourmet catering service for cocktail parties and buffet dinners. In the direct-mail game, the ability to target your audience can be the primary secret of success.

Radio and Television

In terms of radio and television advertising, you need to ask yourself the same kinds of questions as with direct mail. One advantage of radio and television spots over direct mail is that people can't pitch your ad in the wastepaper basket without a glance—although, of course, they may leave the room. And radio and television ads can be less expensive than might be imagined. In smaller cities, for example, it is possible to get a brief television ad produced for under two hundred dollars. Ten seconds of airtime on some programs, repeated eight times in the course of a weekend, can cost as little as one hundred dollars per weekend. But there's often a requirement that you sign a contract for a minimum number of weeks, and that can add up fast.

Unless you have something to show, like crafts or a photo of a buffet spread, it usually makes more sense to use less expensive radio ads than television ads. Radio spots during the morning or evening rush hour might be just the thing for someone who reconditions antique cars or offers a car-washing and hand-polishing service.

As with direct mail, properly targeting your audience is crucial. An ad for handmade dolls could draw considerable response on Nickelodeon on Saturday mornings, but be completely out of place on "Star Trek" reruns. A radio show playing contemporary hit songs is no place for your ad for upscale catering, but might be perfect for special-order T-shirts.

If you are thinking of doing a radio or television ad, you need to listen to a lot of radio and watch a lot of television. Ask your friends and family for advice on what shows might be good to advertise your product or service on. Make a list of possibilities before you talk to the advertising department at a local radio or television station. And keep in mind that the more popular the show, the more an ad is going to cost. Of course, if you have a catering service, you'd like to advertise it on Martha Stewart's show, but you could save a great deal of money and still get results by using the local advertising segment on a less well known but still popular cooking show on the Discovery Channel, or the new Food Channel.

Your Own Web Site?

The majority of at-home businesses are not going to have any need for a Web site on the Internet. There's no point in having national (indeed, worldwide) exposure if your business requires your customers to meet with you face-to-face. Yes, it is possible that someone who lives thirty miles away and hasn't heard of your service or product might discover you on the Internet, and decide to contact you because you live within easy driving distance. But the few such contacts you are liable to generate aren't worth the effort and expense of establishing a Web site.

There are some at-home businesses that might be able to benefit from having a Web site, however. For example, if you've self-published a cookbook (or any kind of book), having a Web site could bring you interest from other parts of the county, and a book can easily be mailed to people, no matter where they live. The same might be true for certain kinds of crafts. But here you have to ask yourself if you are producing enough product to satisfy those who might learn about you on the Internet. Of course, if your business is such a success that you've decided to quit your regular job and devote full time to it, perhaps even hiring employees to work for you, you may well have reached the point where a Web site makes sense—now you will have a lot more product to sell.

If you do want to establish a Web site, you will need to do the same thing you would in placing a local newspaper ad: look at a lot of established Web sites and decide which ones you like and which ones you dislike. Unless you are a very experienced computer hand, you will need to hire a professional to design your Web site. That costs money, but if you have explored the Internet to any real extent, you already know how much information is on it—it's an electronic jungle out there, and your particular site could easily get lost on it. The Internet can offer great opportunities to spread the word about yourself, but don't jump into it without thinking carefully and asking a lot of questions first. Even professionals who own Web-site design companies warn against expecting that a Web site is going to bring you instant riches. They particularly urge that the small business person NOT divert resources from other forms of advertising that are already working well for them.

No matter what advertising medium you are using, remember that a sloppy or badly focused ad isn't going to do you any good no matter where it appears. And even a first-rate ad won't help unless it is specifically tailored to the medium you are using and likely to be seen or heard by people who will have real interest in your particular product or service.

FOUR

125 Home Business Possibilities

Christmas Ornaments

Christmas may come but once a year, but it is the biggest sales season in America. And one of its most obvious and appealing aspects is the sale of Christmas tree ornaments. Every year a few ornaments in every home get broken or are retired because they've faded too much. They make wonderful small presents for anyone who has a tree, as well. And although the market may seem swamped with ornaments, from dime-store cheapies to fifty-dollar works of art by Christopher Radko, there is always room for beautiful imaginative ornaments of all sorts. And some of the nicest you will see are made by people working at home. These days you want to start getting your ornaments to market by September, which means that you start making a given year's supply the previous October.

Astonishing creations can be made by starting with a cheap Sytrofoam base. They can be covered in silk and decorated with gold and silver embroidery, or swatched in glued-on costume jewelry. Hand-sewn animals are always a good seller. Many home-based ornament makers specialize in miniature animals and whimsical figures made entirely out of natural materials, from seed pods to acorns to pinecones. Last year I saw some beautiful hand-painted pinecones, with different bands of color following the natural swirl of the rows of the cone itself.

Depending on the sophistication and beauty of your work, you can easily charge from seven dollars on up to as much as forty dollars for a single ornament, using local boutiques as an outlet or—once your reputation is established—right out of your own home. And don't forget the possibility of creating all the ornaments on a special order for someone who wants a unique tree.

Holiday Decorations

Christmas isn't the only time when people like to give their homes a special holiday feel. Thanksgiving, Easter, Hanukkah, Halloween, Independence Day, Valentine's Day, and even Mother's Day and Father's Day can call for at least some extra effort in the decorating department. And the at-home worker can provide just the thing for all these occasions. Easter baskets, fabulously carved pumpkins, Fourth of July decorations resplendent with small American flags, Pilgrim dioramas—the possibilities are many. And at Christmastime, small, tabletop Christmas trees, fully decorated and lit, can be just the thing for the dining room table, the den, or to give extra warmth to the guest room for holiday visitors.

This kind of work requires imagination and skill in a number of different craft mediums, but the financial rewards can be considerable. People who do this kind of work usually make up a number of different variations on a given holiday theme, since people like to feel that they have a one-of-a-kind decoration. Many find that they are also asked to do special orders, either for special occasions or to incorporate some treasure provided by the customer. Photographs may be used in unique presentations for Mother's and Father's Day or a birthday celebration. A garlanded display stand might show off the wedding photograph and a recent one of a couple celebrating a twenty-fifth or fiftieth wedding anniversary.

You can charge quite variable prices for this kind of decorative display, depending on the amount of work involved. And although you will have to start work for a given holiday well ahead of time, there will be periods when you can take a break for a couple of weeks.

Wreaths Around the Year

When we think of wreaths, we usually picture Christmas wreaths made of evergreens or holly and decorated with pinecones, artificial fruit, and red, green, or gold ribbons. But in many parts of the country, particularly those with Amish and Mennonite populations, from Pennsylvania through Ohio into Indiana, there is a long tradition of having wreaths hung on front doors throughout the year. These are often made from the branches of various kinds of bushes that can be twisted into shape and then dried, with dried flowers, seed pods, and fancy ribbons added as decoration.

In recent years, such year-round wreaths have become popular across the country, and are featured in many mail-order gift, garden, and home-decorating catalogs. But they are often shockingly expensive. If you have a gift for such craftwork, or for making reusable Christmas wreaths that can be brought out year after year, you should have no problem undercutting the prices in mail-order catalogs and making some very good extra cash.

For durable Christmas wreaths, you will probably have to purchase many of the basic materials at craft stores. But if you live in an area that includes open country, you should be able to make trips into the countryside to collect the branches and seed pods used in constructing year-round wreaths. That means extra profits. This can be a very creative and satisfying at-home job, and you could hardly choose one with greater word-of-mouth possibilities, since your creations will be prominently displayed on the front door of your customers' homes.

Dried Flower Arrangements

There are few things nicer than fresh flower arrangements, but few of us can afford to have them except on special occasions unless we're lucky enough to have a sizable flower garden—and that will still leave us bereft in the winter months. For that reason, dried flower arrangements have become increasingly popular in recent years. If you have a gift for flower arranging—and even with dried flowers, the combination used and the way they are put together can make a great deal of difference—consider the possibility of making dried arrangements for sale.

There are numerous flowers that dry beautifully, from standards such as bachelor's buttons and hydrangeas to exotic possibilities such as the graceful pods known as kangaroo's toes. Most flowers that dry well simply need to be hung upside down in bunches in a cool, well-ventilated place for a week or so. They can then be arranged in bouquets of different heights and sizes. Some customers may prefer to buy an arrangement to display in one of their own vases, but a higher price can be charged by providing a vase or wicker basket as well. When a container is included, the arrangements make wonderful gifts for many occasions at all times of the year.

Papier-Mâché

The art of papier-mâché (a French term that in America is usually pronounced simply as "paper mashay") has been in existence for centuries. The wonderful thing about this art form is that it is so inexpensive. Wire screening, wallpaper paste, and sheets of newspaper put you in business. The screening is simply bent into the desired sculptural shape, and then layers of newspaper and paste are applied to build up the form. After applying a coat or two of paint primer, you're ready to do the decorative painting.

The shapes you construct can be simple vases and urns, any kind of animal or bird, even human faces and torsos. Some artists make whimsical variants on appliances such as toasters or television sets, or create extraordinary hats or masks. I have seen papier-mâché chili peppers ranging in size from six inches to three feet, not to mention a bust of Madonna with arms flung up to the heavens as Evita Perón. Because papier-mâché is such a pliable medium, many artists specialize in amusing items such as a cow jumping over the moon, or the Owl and the Pussycat afloat in their boat—perfect decorations for a child's room.

Many gift shops are happy to take papier-mâché items

on consignment because they look great in shop windows, attracting the attention of passersby—which also gives your work pride of place. In fact, once a papier-mâché artist gets known in a community, it often happens that other stores commission pieces simply to be used as window displays.

Dolls for Sale

Remember the extraordinary craze for Cabbage Patch Dolls a few years ago? The man who created them did so at home, sold them locally, and suddenly found major toy companies bidding to buy the rights to his idea. Nobody knows where the next such craze is going to come from in the world of dolls, but you can be sure that somebody out there, starting in his or her own living room or kitchen, will eventually make a small fortune. Fortunes aside, there is a steady market for clever or pretty homemade dolls.

Some people in this line of work started making dolls for their own amusement and began selling them in response to the enthusiasm of friends and family. Others, who knew from the start that they wanted to establish a home-based business, deliberately gave a number of dolls away to get started, realizing that all that's necessary to create demand is a few children having a doll that's different and that other children want. One woman remembers that when she got a telephone call from a friend saying that the neighbor's daughter had stolen the doll given to her daughter by this doll-maker, she knew her business was about to take off.

There are all kinds of dolls that people make at home to sell, from cloth creations with hand-painted faces to dolls put together from purchased heads and hands but dressed to the nines. Most home doll-makers find that there are two or three favorites they make that go on selling year after year, but even so, they regularly create new styles in the hope that one of them may turn out to be a success story like the Cabbage Patch Doll.

Dollhouse Furniture

All you have to do is look at the gift catalogs from museums these days to see that there is a considerable vogue for elegant dollhouse furniture. You will see examples of Louis XVI, Chippendale, and high Victorian furniture, minuscule in size but as complexly carved and decorated as full-size originals. Such furniture is, of course, bought for actual dollhouses—it makes great Christmas presents for grandchildren—but many people, men as well as women, collect miniature furniture, which they display in glass-fronted cases. The market for miniature furniture has always existed to a degree, but has expanded greatly in the last decade.

This is delicate, time-consuming work, requiring great skill and patience, but the financial rewards can be considerable. Single pieces of particularly ornate dollhouse furniture often sell for thirty-five to seventy-five dollars. If you have the talent for this kind of work, consider creating a Web page on the Internet to advertise your work. It is in demand not only for dollhouses and by collectors of miniatures, but also can be required for unusual purposes, such as in advertising and even for use in special-effects scenes in movies. In that kind of situation, very specific pieces may be needed to replicate actual full-size furniture used in the film, and such commissioned work can fetch extraordinary prices. In general, if you are asked to re-create a specific piece in miniature, do not hesitate to ask for a lot of money.

Decorative Eggs

The egg shape has always been one of the most pleasing to the human eye, and decorated eggs have always played their part in the cultural history of the world, from the hard-boiled eggs we color at Easter to the breathtaking jeweled masterpieces created by the great Russian gold-smith Peter Carl Fabergé for the czars. There are folk-art nesting wooden eggs, marble eggs, glass eggs, and hand-carved stone eggs to be found in shops and homes around the world.

Decorated eggs can take many forms. Blown eggs, using ancient techniques for removing the yolks and whites from eggshells, can be decorated whimsically or with pre-cise geometric patters, sold as year-round decorative ob-jects or angled toward Easter or Christmas holiday giving. Wooden or stone eggs can be treated to the same breadth of decorative styles. I have seen papier-mâché eggs—the unpainted, light-as-a-feather egg forms can be bought at most craft stores—made to look like lustrous marble or given an elegance to rival museum pieces. An artist of my acquaintance uses Styrofoam egg forms onto which he glues tiny seashells and metal trimmings to make min-iature masterpieces for which collectors pay one hundred dollars each.

If you have artistic ability, decorating eggs can be a real moneymaker at several different levels of expertise.

Painted Rocks

Go ahead and laugh, but rocks are making a comeback—and that doesn't mean the jokey "pet rock" of twenty-five years ago. Artists are doing extraordinary things with rocks these days. From hand-painted jewelry to paperweights to garden sculptures, decorative rocks are big sellers. Small rocks can be painted and turned into pins or necklaces with supplies from craft stores. Larger rocks, either singly or hot-glued together into sculptural formations, make great paperweights. And behemoths weighing several pounds can be seen gracing many gardens or used in the house as doorstops.

Flowers and geometric or abstract designs can be seen on rocks used for jewelry or paperweights. Animals, from cat faces to frogs, bears, wolves, and birds, turn up on paperweights and garden pieces. When painted by an accomplished artist, these pieces can sell for $15 to $125, depending on size and beauty. Many artists working in this medium get their rocks for free at the seashore or along the sides of country roads. Nature provides both polished little gems and larger hunks in exotic shapes. You can often buy a supply of rocks quite cheaply from landscaping companies as well.

Some rock painters sell their rocks on a consignment basis through gift stores; signed garden pieces are offered by many mail-order companies. But other artists find that the best way to sell their wares is to set up a table at a flea market, with finished pieces ready for sale while the artist paints new ones on site. A working artist always draws a crowd, and can sometimes lead to special orders for future delivery as well. In the latter case, be sure to get a down payment.

Painted Boxes

Everyone likes handsomely decorated boxes. Not only are they nice objects in themselves, but you can put things in them, getting the endless clutter of life stashed away out of sight but easily found. You'll see boxes of every shape and size, and decorated to suit every taste—including no taste—at flea markets, town fairs, and upscale boutiques and antique shops. They make great gifts, because they're personal without being too personal, and anyone is glad to get one, men as well as women. And children love them.

For the home artist, boxes are a nice thing to work on because they can be decorated a section at a time, and since many of the best designs involve layered effects, drying time is needed in between work sessions. They're not something you have to finish at a single work session. In fact, most people who specialize in painting boxes have several going at once in different stages of completion.

Wooden boxes in many shapes are available in raw form at crafts store, but some people in this field can do wonders giving new life to commercial boxes, including cigar boxes and those that smoked salmon and dried cod are shipped in. Commercial boxes are best used by artists who like to paint in layers, since it is often necessary to obscure the brand names stamped into the wood.

Boxes accommodate many styles of painting, from landscapes and still lifes to geometric designs and faux-marble effects. Seashells, costume jewelry beads, and dried leaves or seed pods can be hot-glued to a box. The price you charge depends on how much work went into the box and how beautiful it is.

Commemorative Plates

Thousands of commemorative plates are issued every year by commercial plate manufacturers to mark historic anniversaries, winning sports teams, state fairs, and the like. And then there are collectors' plates celebrating famous movies such as *The Wizard of Oz* or *Gone With the Wind.* But you can take advantage of the popularity of commemorative plates by creating ones that the big commercial companies wouldn't deal with. That means hand-painted plates to celebrate twenty-fifth or fiftieth wedding anniversaries, the birth of a child, kids' graduations from high school or college, or dozens of other special occasions unique to individual families.

To do well in this line of work, you need to be good at lettering, and it helps a great deal to be able to do portraits as well—the smiling faces of Grandpa and Grandma on a fiftieth-anniversary plate can mean that several members of the family may want their own keepsake. This is a very strong word-of-mouth service—once you've established yourself, ads will become unnecessary unless you want to expand to a mail-order service, which would mean turning this sideline into a full-time job and probably hiring additional people to do the painting. But you can do very nicely on a small scale with this business, as a strictly part-time endeavor.

Pressed Flowers

This is a hobby that can bring in a nice amount of extra cash. The late Princess Grace of Monaco not only made gorgeous framed creations from pressed flowers, but also wrote a book on the subject. Not that she needed the money, of course, but you can generate some useful cash for yourself by pressing flowers and leaves, and then constructing artful collages by gluing the dried results to stiff backings and framing them.

Pressed-flower pictures are a terrific artistic outlet for people who have a strong sense of design and color but little ability to draw. Delicate dried ferns, rose petals with a subtle hint of their original color, and brighter accents of flowers or leaves that retain deeper shades even when dried can make for a stunning and original composition.

Flower presses are widely available for reasonable prices, and there are numerous good books on special techniques for both drying and mounting nature's bounty. Quite aside from the fact that dried-flower pictures are very popular and can bring good money, the collection of the raw materials encourages many pleasurable and healthy hours wandering in parks, fields, and woods. And if you have a garden of your own, it will provide an enormous amount of material that keeps right on giving pleasure even when the garden itself is buried under a foot of snow.

Birdhouses

Crazes come and go, but hand-painted birdhouses seem to be here to stay. They can serve as an indoor decoration or be used for their rightful purpose hanging from a tree limb in the backyard. Raw-wood birdhouses can be bought for a reasonable price at almost any large arts and crafts store. It's what you do to them that determines their value on the market.

Hand-painted flowers and fruit are always popular, as

are amusing conceits such as showing a golf ball rolling across a green front, with the entrance hole representing the golf cup. They can be painted to look like miniature human habitats, complete with glued-on shutters. Christmas motifs are always a good bet in the early winter. Many birdhouses one sees for sale in catalogs or gift shops are simply cute. But the highest-priced ones are works of art, beauties that stop people in their tracks.

If you have any skills as a carpenter, constructing your own birdhouses can pay off, since unusual shapes command higher prices. A jack-o'-lantern front for Halloween, or a snowman at Christmas, can be a real winner. Many gift shops are willing to sell birdhouses on a consignment basis, with the shop taking a percentage of the sale price and the creator getting the rest. Most shops will take about 40 percent.

You can make more money for yourself, in many cases, by displaying your wares at flea markets or fairs, avoiding the middleman. If you have the ability to produce birdhouses so pretty that they become a "must-have" item instead of just an impulse buy, you may be able to get a mail-order catalog to feature your creations, at prices ranging up to seventy-five dollars.

Seashell Frames

If you live near the ocean, don't just admire the hundreds of seashells that get washed up on the beach. Bend over, pick up the perfect ones, and take them home. Buy simple wooden frames, acquire an inexpensive glue gun, and set to work. If you have a good sense of design, it is possible to make lovely creations quite quickly and sell them at a considerable profit. Tourist shops always have large supplies of such frames, and they often acquire them from local artisans who do the work in their spare time.

Some people who do this kind of work simply turn out a great many of these frames as quickly as possible. They're pretty but more in the nature of souvenirs than works of art. There are individuals who take this craft to a higher plane, however, creating larger and more ornate frames that are exquisite examples of the frame-maker's art. This kind of work isn't usually available in the regular tourist shops but is sold instead in high-end boutiques for much higher prices. Frames of this sort are likely to be used for mirrors and prominently displayed in people's homes. Some examples sell for as much as $150–$250.

Pottery

Beautiful hand-thrown pottery never goes out of style. From priceless museum pieces thousands of years old to thousand-dollar creations of major contemporary artists, pottery has always been a cherished decorative (and often practical) medium of expression. What's more, its appeal crosses all lines of taste and expense, from whimsical coffee mugs to elegant bowls and vases that grace the most elite dinner parties.

The famously sexy scene of Patrick Swayze and Demi Moore nuzzling over a pottery wheel in the hit movie *Ghost* gave the sales of pottery and enrollment in pottery classes a big boost that has continued ever since. Inexpensive pottery can be seen at every fair and flea market, and fine pieces are regularly a feature at exhibitions of contemporary crafts in museums around the country. At whatever level you work, your pottery can make you money, whether it be a little "mad money" from cute coffee mugs, or substantial income from the kind of sophisticated and gorgeous pottery that wins prizes at art exhibitions.

Mobiles

Mobiles are very popular. You see all kinds of constructions hanging from people's ceilings: every sort of bird, from brilliantly colored parrots to elegant white cranes, groupings of old airplanes, wildly imaginative spaceships, jungle animals, seashell shapes, the planets of the solar system, and many others.

Most mobiles on the market are made from heavy paper, with designs on both sides, of course, so that they show themselves to good advantage no matter which way they turn. And turn they must. The heavy thread, light cord, or thin wire that holds the various elements of the mobile suspended must be of varying lengths, so the figures can revolve without crashing into one another. Most mobiles are made so that they can be folded up and packaged, but the instructions for putting them together at home have to be crystal-clear. That often means that each different design must have instructions unique to it. Of course, you can design a mobile and have many copies of it printed up.

More expensive mobiles are also made from metal, light wood, and even seashells. These are more durable and can usually be classified as unique works of art—which means that they carry much higher prices.

Stained Glass

Numerous people with an artistic bent and a talent for putting things together have gotten interested in stained-glass ornaments, taken classes, and then gone on to develop a lucrative little business selling the decorative pieces they make. There are shops that sell glass by the piece, as well as the soldering tools and material, all over the country. In many cases, such shops will also sell an artist's work on a consignment basis, although it is certainly worthwhile to advertise as well and sell pieces directly from your home.

Small stained-glass pieces in various shapes that can be hung in windows to catch the light have become extremely popular in recent years. Butterfly, bird, and flower ornaments of this kind are always in demand, as are seasonal ornaments such as pumpkins and Christmas trees or stars. Some stained-glass artisans also make a specialty of pieces that feature names, logos of college or professional sports teams, or coats of arms. While hanging ornaments sell particularly fast, some artists have been successful with larger pieces that are mounted on free-standing bases. The truly proficient artist may even move on to major pieces such as lampshades and fan windows for over front doors. This is a field in which one can start small and go on to more expensive pieces as the customer base and the artist's own expertise grow over time.

Custom-Made Lampshades

Lampshades come in a wide variety of styles, ranging from the conical drum to the Oriental "pagoda" shape, and in fabrics ranging from parchment paper to the finest silk or brocade. Yet people often go looking for the perfect shade for an unusual lamp and come up empty-handed or find themselves settling for something that is okay but not exactly right. That frustration creates a niche market for custom-made lampshades.

This is not an easy job. It requires the ability to make the metal frame for the shade—although old frames can sometimes be recycled with a fresh coat of metallic paint—to cut and stitch or glue a wide variety of shade materials, and sometimes that special knack for understanding what a customer wants even when he or she can't quite put it into words. But it is also a lucrative business. Good lampshades are expensive, and the kind of people willing to go the custom-made route invariably have money to spend and are willing to pay what's necessary to get just what they want.

Personalized Lamps

This one is fun. There has been a vogue in recent years for making lamps out of unusual objects. Antique gumball machines, 1930s cookie jars, dolls, Disney statuettes, and a host of other oddities have been turned into lamps. Perhaps these usually humorous, sometimes sentimental, and occasionally beautiful creations appeal to people as a kind of defiant gesture against an increasingly homogenized world.

Making lamps out of curious objects is not just a matter of knowing how to do electrical wiring. Mounting these objects requires real ingenuity and a considerable range of crafts skills. But a simple ad in the local paper has brought many people a surprising flow of customers bear-

ing objects dredged out of their attics or basements—
objects they didn't know quite what to do with but
couldn't bring themselves to throw away.

And since these lamps are inevitably great conversation
pieces, word of mouth is likely to bring you many other
customers, who see one of your creations and think, Hey,
that's what I can do with that funny old triangular toaster.
Be prepared for almost anything: One of the home-decoration
magazines recently featured a lamp made from a pair of
what looked like the world's oldest pair of cowboy boots.
Price? Five hundred dollars.

Bookcases

It would seem that there are plenty of bookcases on the
market, from thousand-dollar rare-wood models to the
fiberboard kind that comes in a box to be assembled at home.
But there are many people who can't afford mahogany, yet
want something more substantial and better-looking than fiberboard. Good commercial wooden bookcases are available, but they are surprisingly expensive, especially if
there are shipping costs involved. What's more, many
people want to have a bookcase that exactly fits a particular space in their homes, and it can be difficult or impossi-
ble to find one that fills the bill.

Are you a good carpenter? Numerous people have
found that they can make excellent money in this kind of
work. It's an at-home job that can bring in extra cash in
almost any community, but if there is any kind of college
in your area, you are likely to do an especially good business. It won't come from the students but rather the fac-
ulty, who will have large collections of books and who
care about how they are shelved and shown off.

The one catch in this kind of business is that you really should have a van and be able to hire the occasional helper, since most people are going to want to have their bookcases delivered. Of course, you will include the cost of doing that in the prices you charge. Prices are usually determined by the kind of wood the customer wants as well as the kind of finish—whether stained or in some particular color to match their woodwork or walls—by size, and by how much decorative molding the customer may want.

Bookends

Not all books belong in bookcases. Many people like to display certain books as a decorative accent on tabletops or mantels. Big coffee-table books can be laid flat and still look impressive, but smaller books with particularly nice bindings look much better if they are standing upright between a pair of handsome bookends. Museum shops and catalogs usually have bookends that are scaled-down representations of sculptures in their collections. But these can be quite expensive. There is a niche market for hand-crafted bookends which can be made at home and sold for less money.

Bookends can be made from numerous materials, including hand-carved wood, papier-mâché, painted rocks, or even mounted figurines of various kinds. Painted rocks have sufficient weight on their own to hold up several books, but in many cases it will be necessary to weight the base on which the decorative element is mounted. Papier-mâché forms can be filled with pebbles as well. There is no end to the possible decorative motifs that can be employed, from animals to masks to fanciful abstract constructions.

Many people who do this kind of work add to their income, and attract additional customers, by mounting objects provided by the customer to serve as bookends. They are brought everything from old china cookie jars to bronzed baby shoes and asked to turn them into bookends. Your own creations can often be sold on a consignment basis through local gift stores, but there's nothing like customized bookends to bring you good word of mouth.

Hand-Painted Furniture

Hand-painted furniture has been in and out of vogue throughout American history. Examples from the nineteenth century now bring high prices on the antiques market, although a couple of decades ago you could hardly give them away. Hand-painted chairs and chests have never gone out of style in some parts of the country, such as Pennsylvania Dutch country, but they are now enjoying a national revival. You see them—at very high prices—in many home-furnishing catalogs, and they are often featured in the homes shown in home decorating magazines.

If you have a gift for landscapes, flowers, and animals, or are good at stencil work, there will be a very strong market for your talents at the present time. Some people who do this kind of work buy old furniture at flea markets and junk stores, strip it down, and then repaint it in fanciful designs. Others buy fairly good-quality unfinished new furniture and work on it. The colors of most hand-painted furniture are soft, with lots of pastel blues, greens, and rose hues. Gold accenting is popular.

This is meticulous but very creative work. Depending to some extent on the quality of the basic piece of furniture, but more on the skill of the artist, such pieces can sell for as much as several hundred dollars. And who knows? Your work may someday become a treasured antique itself.

Whimsical Tables

You've undoubtedly seen them, in a magazine or catalog or in someone's house—small tables cut into shapes that suggest various animals, from turtles to zebras, or chairs with backs that have been cut in the shape of giraffe's necks. Brightly painted, these whimsical creatures make great room accents and conversation pieces. They were first produced by two or three well-known artists, but now a great many artisans are getting into this area, including people who make them at home in their spare time.

You can certainly create these tables and side chairs using motifs you've seen elsewhere, giving them your own twist, but if you can come up with some fresh ideas, you can probably charge higher prices. How about chairs cut into the shapes of various kinds of space aliens? Characters from children's books that are in the public domain, such as *Alice's Adventures in Wonderland* and the Oz books, could be a big success in small sizes for children's rooms. But stay away from Dr. Seuss or Disney characters, since you could run into copyright problems.

Masks

This is an unusual but very creative at-home job that can take two different forms. Some people specialize in masks to be worn, while others make decorative masks to be hung on the wall. Masks for wearing are produced for Halloween, of course, as well as for costume parties, special occasions, and sometimes for local theater groups. Masks to be hung on the wall or displayed on a table are in essence pieces of sculpture.

Masks to be worn must be reasonably comfortable and allow for proper breathing, and can be constructed of cloth, paper, or even of latex if the artist is willing to invest in the molds and heating units necessary for that kind of work. Wall masks can be made from a greater variety of materials, including clay, wood, plaster of paris, pottery, and metal. But in both kinds of creations, a fanciful imagination plays a major role.

Generally speaking, Halloween and other wearable masks must be priced affordably, since many of them will be bought for children, but people who work in this field occasionally get a special order for an adult special-occasion mask for which the customer is willing to pay as much as $150–$200. Sculptural masks, on the other hand, because they are made to last, out of sometimes expensive materials, can regularly be priced at a much higher level.

Marionettes and Hand Puppets

Handmade wooden marionettes are not necessarily a toy for children. Many people collect them, and even when bought singly, they can serve as a decorative accent or conversation piece. Some marionette-makers concentrate on a specialty such as figures of United States presidents—there is a considerable market for a likeness of Ronald Reagan or Bill Clinton that can be made to dance at the owner's will at the end of strings!

Some such marionettes are quite simple in construction and can be made from balsa wood. A cutout magazine photograph can serve as a face, preserved under clear shellac. More sophisticated marionettes are hand-carved works of art. There is a Virginia couple who collaborate on making marionettes. The husband is a surgeon with a gift for wood carving, who constructs and carves the bodies, with movable arms and legs and hand-carved faces, in his workshop. He then turns them over to his wife, an advertising executive by profession, who paints the figures and does the stringing. They charge one hundred dollars and up for their marionettes, and will create special orders—recently a computer store owner commissioned one of Bill Gates.

Some marionette-makers sell their creations with costumes painted on; others sew elaborate bejeweled cloth costumes. On a much simpler level, hand puppets without strings can be made entirely out of cloth. One woman uses bright-colored socks bought at closeout sales, with faces made from buttons and small craft items; tufts of wool are used for hair, and ribbon for costume accents. She can make several of these an hour, and at five dollars apiece, they are much in demand as party favors for both children and adults.

Scarecrows

Don't laugh. There are craftspeople who get from sixty dollars to one hundred dollars for each scarecrow they make. These aren't figures to put into the cornfield—farmers know how to make those for themselves. You will sometimes find one of these whimsical creatures reposing on a wrought-iron bench in a corner of the garden, however. They also put in appearances in family rooms, dens, and big eat-in kitchens. But wherever they spend most of their time hanging out, they are likely to show up on the porch or in the front hall at Halloween.

These are decorative scarecrows, friendly spirits with smiling faces that people like to have around for company, or to provoke amusement from guests. (Now, it's okay to laugh.) Many are actually stuffed with straw, but cotton wadding and packaging foam are also used. The heads, hands, and feet are shaped and sewn, and the faces hand-painted.

Some are male, some female; there are even kid-sized scarecrows. I know a family who commissioned a scarecrow artist to make one resembling each member of the family, Mom, Dad, and all four kids. They're dressed in clothes each member of the family actually wore, and are to be found gathered at one end of the small barn that has been turned into a large family room. There are moments when, out of the corner of your eye, you could swear you just caught them moving.

Portraits

If you have a talent for painting or drawing the human face, put it to work for you. Yes, of course, your family and friends appreciate the portraits you do of them as birthday or Christmas presents—in fact, haven't they been saying, "You could make money doing this"? Well, you certainly can.

Thousands of artists across the country make lots of extra money doing portraits in various mediums—oil or acrylic paint, pastels, charcoal, and even watercolor. Don't be afraid to display your own particular style in portraits; that, after all, is what makes them unique and thus more treasured than most commercial photographs.

Some people may be willing to "sit" in person for a fairly elaborate portrait. But often someone will want to give a portrait of a spouse, parent, or friend to that person as a surprise, which will mean working from a photograph. And that is usually the best idea anyway when doing portraits of children, which are particularly popular. You can change the background, and even the clothing, to give the portrait a more formal look. (Many of the nineteenth-century portraits seen in people's homes, and even in museums, were done by itinerant painters who went door to door with canvases that were already painted except for the face and hands, which were then done from life quite quickly.)

Depending on the size and complexity of a portrait, as well as the medium it is done in and the level of skill you possess, prices can range from fifty dollars to several hundred. And many artists who have started locally have eventually advertised in national magazines.

Portraits of Pets

Most artists find they have a particular affinity for one kind of artwork. It may be portraits, it may be landscapes. But artists can also surprise themselves. One Boston artist, for example, who had sold both landscapes and portraits, was asked by a friend to do a portrait of her purebred Afghan hound. The artist agreed somewhat reluctantly, but then found to his surprise that the resulting dog portrait turned out to be one of the best paintings he'd ever done.

Some artists would have chalked this up as a fluke, but he decided to pursue this new direction. Within a year he had one of his portraits on the cover of a dog magazine, and found himself with a steady stream of customers who were willing to pay several hundred dollars to have their dogs immortalized. For the first time, the artist found himself making enough money from his painting sideline that he seriously considered quitting his "day job."

That's a special case, but there is definitely money to be made in portraits of pets, cats as much as dogs. Because pets are even worse at posing than young children, most pet artists work from photographs, insisting upon at least eight-by-ten blowups, since snapshots are difficult to use. Since this is commissioned work, such artists draw up specific contracts and require a down payment. If the customer wants the painting already framed, a charge for that is included also, and special arrangements can often be arrived at between the artist and a professional frame shop. As with portraits of people, a little flattery will get you everywhere when painting a pet, and bring in new commissions as well.

Caricatures

Al Hirshfeld's famous caricatures have been gracing the pages of *The New York Times* and the walls of New York's famed Sardi's restaurant for more than half a century. But you don't have to have his legendary facility and finesse to make some extra money doing this kind of artwork. Many people have a gift for simple line drawings that, by slightly exaggerating people's physical appearance, bring a smile to the face.

If you're the kind of person who doodles this kind of drawing on paper napkins or in the margins of notebooks, think about the possibility of making some money with this talent. Caricatures make terrific birthday presents. With a good clear photograph, the artist can capture a person's face in a few lines, and add whatever touches the presenter wishes.

For example, I have friends who have caricatures of each of them framed on the bathroom wall. The wife is dressed as a parody of the *Mona Lisa*, while the husband, who has a beard, appears as Vincent Van Gogh, with a missing ear. Many guests who have seen the drawings have asked how to get in touch with the artist, and ordered pictures for themselves. This is not so much a case of word-of-mouth advertising as of "to see one is to want one."

Photographs for Greeting Cards

Do you take terrific photographs of flowers, landscapes, local historic buildings, or animals? Many fine photographers who have professional skills but take photographs largely as a hobby have found that they can make extra money by having multiple copies made of their best photographs and mounting them on plain folding cards that they buy in bulk at wholesale prices, together with the envelopes for the cards. No message has to be printed on the inside—in fact, many buyers will prefer having a blank card because it is adaptable to any occasion.

Go around to all the local gift shops that have cards for sale. Many will be delighted to sell cards by a local photographer on a consignment basis. Local art galleries can also be a good outlet for your work. While you may not make a profit of more than fifty cents on a card that sells for $1.25 (after costs and the shop's commission), that can mount up surprisingly. It is quite common for people who get into this business to eventually acquire national distribution for their work, particularly through mail-order gift catalogs. Such companies are always looking for new cards to offer, since they help to give a fresh look to new catalogs at minimal expense.

Special-Occasion Signs

While driving around town, have you ever noticed a special sign in a front yard? "Happy Birthday, Betty," it might read. Or "Happy 50th Anniversary to Bob and Irene." Or "Welcome Home, Eric." Somebody made these signs, and the sign-maker is seldom a person who lives in the house.

If you have a gift for hand-lettering, or are good at using stencils, this is a nice way to make some extra money. Signs marking special occasions are a way for people to give a little extra spark to a celebration in a very American apple-pie kind of way. Once you get started in this business, you'll find that every sign of yours that goes up will bring in new customers who think it's a neat idea.

If you can also make cloth banners, for inside or outside use, it will expand your business. It's also a good idea to have a supply of signs for rent for certain occasions—yard sales, parking signs for weddings or big parties, even signs that urge victory for a local football team. Some people who do this work find that they eventually get regular contracts to provide the signs for municipal events such as town fairs. This kind of work isn't going to make you rich, but it can bring in a surprising amount of extra cash, and it's a "feel good" endeavor that will put smiles on a lot of faces.

Advertising Posters

This is a particularly good way for someone with artistic ability and a good graphic sense to make extra money at home. You'll find there are many potential clients at the local level who don't want to invest in hiring an advertising firm but need promotional posters. Small businesses, shops, clubs, and churches all may need a poster on occasion. And don't forget about fledgling rock or rap groups, local theaters, or kids' sports teams.

Color reproduction has become much cheaper in recent years, but some clients may still want to stick with the even less expensive black-and-white poster, so be sure to have samples of both kinds to show off. It's also important to offer a variety of sizes. A good poster can make money for your client, so don't hesitate to charge $75–$150 for your work, depending on how complicated the job is. Your name should certainly appear in small print in a lower corner of the poster, and try to persuade clients to let you put your telephone number next to it. They'll usually be willing if you suggest giving them a slightly lower rate if they allow you to advertise yourself in this way.

As people who do this kind of work establish a reputation, they sometimes discover that a client wants a poster that can be sold for a few dollars to poster collectors. If this situation arises, negotiate a small royalty on such sales, drawing up a contract that covers the details of the agreement and having it notarized. Even fifty cents a poster can add substantially to your income over time.

Hand-Carved and Hand-Painted Signs

Businesses in many parts of the country, especially in areas that draw tourists, like to draw attention to their restaurants and shops with hand-painted or hand-carved signs that hang out front. A good sign of this sort not only attracts attention but suggests quality. In the days before neon, such signs were to be found everywhere, and have always been prevalent in old-fashioned cities like New Orleans. But they have been making a big comeback in recent years as an alternative to electric signs, which sometimes aren't even allowed in the historic districts of many towns and smaller cities.

Wooden signs cut in distinctive shapes and simply hand-painted are the easiest to produce, and even these can command good prices when the artist has a flair for color and lettering. But the top of the line in this field is hand-carved signs in which the lettering is incised into the wood and then painted or, often, lined with gold leaf. This kind of sign often makes tourists stop and take a photograph—and often enter the shop or restaurant as well.

When well-made and thoroughly weatherproofed, hand-painted and hand-carved signs can last for years, and may even improve in looks as the elements take their toll. Because such signs are regarded by businesspeople as a fundamental investment, they are willing to pay very good prices for high-quality results. A hand-carved sign in particular may bring several hundred dollars.

Personalized Mailboxes

In suburban areas, a great many people like to put a stamp of individuality on their property by having a personalized mailbox. They're fun, they look a lot better than standard-issue metal mailboxes, and they can be handy signposts when giving people directions on how to get to your house. "Turn onto Maple Drive and look for the mailbox in the shape of a steamboat!"

Personalized mailboxes can take a great many different shapes and forms, from boats to birdcages to sunflowers. Some people like to have a mailbox that is a miniature version of the house they live in. If you're good at carpentry, this is an enjoyable and surprisingly lucrative side business. The mail-order catalogs are full of personalized mailboxes these days, and many of them cost a pretty penny. But the only difference between one mailbox bought from a catalog and another will be the name. If you can offer really individual examples, you can charge just as much, or even more, than the mail-order businesses do.

Homemade Pies, Cheesecakes, and Bread

All over the country, there are kitchens filled with the wonderful aromas of fresh-baked pies, cheesecakes, and breads—but they're not being baked for a family occasion. The women (and men) doing the baking are involved in making extra money. And they have no shortage of customers. As foods become more and more processed, and as what some people refer to as the "food police" have reached the point of declaring almost everything but grains, vegetables, and fruit bad for us, a backlash has set in. Many people want old-fashioned pies with butter crusts, real cheesecakes that feel like something substantial on the fork, and breads with texture and character.

The cooks who specialize in these fresh-baked products usually start out by baking on weekends only. They begin Friday evening and spend several hours Saturday morning baking, taking a break in the afternoon, and start in again Saturday night, with some final work done early Sunday morning. Everything is usually sold out by 1:00 P.M. as people stop by to pick up their orders, or to see what's available, after church on Sunday, and the baker can relax for the rest of the day.

Once word has spread about these old-fashioned goodies, there are plenty of customers. Most bakers take orders over the phone, preparing only as many pies, cakes, or breads as have been requested in advance, with maybe one for the family and an extra in case somebody shows up who doesn't know the order-in-advance routine. Pies are snapped up at thirteen to twenty-two dollars, depending on the expense of the fruit that goes into them, cheesecakes start at about twenty dollars, and breads go for about half as much.

Decorated Cookies

First-rate pastry shops always have decorated cookies for sale, some of them so beautiful that they look almost too good to eat—but not quite! But such pastry shops have a high overhead, and many people who would otherwise like to buy such cookies for parties or special family occasions blanche at paying $1.75 for a single cookie. The pastry whiz who works from home can undercut the price of the pastry shops and also offer the possibility of making personalized cookies for the individual client.

As those who follow the comic strip "Blondie" will be aware, when Blondie started her catering service a few years back, her main problem turned out to be Dagwood's appetite. Making decorated cookies is *not* a good sideline for those with young children in the house. The author knows one woman who started making decorated cookies for sale after the youngest child went off to college. Her kids had always been so thrilled with her cookies that she missed the pleasure of their responses when they left home. Now she has the satisfaction of people calling her up and saying they'd had her cookies at a party, gotten her number from the hostess, and just had to have some themselves. And unlike her kids, her delighted customers pay her for the privilege of baking her small masterpieces.

Wedding Cakes

If making wedding cakes sounds like a very specialized business, you're quite correct—but that's just what makes it lucrative. Many professional pastry chefs, people who work at the finest restaurants, can turn out desserts that have people swooning, yet don't want to have anything to do with making wedding cakes. It's not just that the cake must taste good and look fabulous, but it must also have a consistency that makes it slice extremely easily. Beyond that, the several tiers of a wedding cake require an architectural understanding that goes beyond culinary skill.

Famous bakeries in major cities always have someone on the staff who specializes in making wedding cakes. But in the last fifteen years or so, hundreds of people across the country have gone into business for themselves doing nothing but creating wedding cakes, often working out of their own homes. Many such entrepreneurs have discovered that they have a special talent for wedding cakes almost by accident. Known for their baking skills, they may be asked to prepare a wedding cake for a friend on a budget, and realize that they really have a knack for this difficult task. If you're a good baker and looking for a way to make some extra money, experiment with a few wedding cakes. It could be the path to substantial extra income. For a large wedding, many people are willing to spend several hundred dollars on a spectacular cake.

Home Canning

The oldest indoor farmer's market in continuous operation in America is in Lancaster, Pennsylvania. In existence since the 1870s, it is a huge, airy brick structure packed with dozens of stalls selling everything from produce to meat and fish to fancy baked goods. Numerous stalls sell home-canned delicacies produced by Amish and Mennonite farmers' wives in their big home kitchens. Jams, jellies, pickles, horseradish, and mustards are arrayed in sparkling glass jars with pretty or whimsical labels. They're expensive, but tourists buy them in great quantities, and locals aren't immune, either.

Did you learn home canning at your mother's or grandmother's knee, or simply become expert at it on your own? Your delicacies can make you a surprising amount of money. Taste is important in this endeavor, of course, but not only in terms of being delicious on the tongue. Attractive labels are a crucial ingredient in the sale of these foods. At the Lancaster market, many labels are still done by hand—these families always seem to have someone with an artistic gift—and the tops often have small rounds of chintz or checkered cloth attached between the sealing round and the screw top. But color reproduction has become so good and so inexpensive that there's no reason why a special label can't be run off in quantity.

Even if there is no farmer's market in your area, gift, kitchenware, and food shops are usually happy to take these lovely products on consignment. Any local specialty—from beach-plum jelly on Cape Cod to chowchow in Pennsylvania—will sell particularly well to tourists.

Bottled Vinegars and Infused Oils

In recent years, as Americans have become more and more open to fancy and unusual foods, a strong market has developed for fancy vinegars with branches of herbs right in the bottle, as well as for olive and other oils that have been infused with the essence of lemons, oranges, raspberries, cranberries, and all kinds of herbs and spices.

As with home canning, presentation is important with these gourmet items. A lovely label is a big help, but the bottle itself can be far more important than with jars of jelly or pickles. There are a great many special bottles available these days, imported from the Mediterranean countries in particular, that can greatly increase your sales of bottled vinegars or infused oils. They are not always inexpensive, but can often be bought in bulk wholesale. And of course, their price is included in what you charge. People often buy these homemade products as much for the bottles as for what is in them, and are willing to pay as much as seventeen to twenty-two dollars for a large bottle.

Home-Grown Herbs

Even the best supermarkets carry only a modest selection of fresh herbs, and to the shopper it may always seem that the one they really need for a recipe isn't available when they want it. In addition, fresh herbs don't keep very well— which is why supermarkets are loath to sock them in any quantity or variety. That leaves a real opening for the individual with a green thumb and the space in the backyard to establish a substantial herb garden. Customers are willing to pay premium prices for fresh herbs exactly because they are hard to come by.

Those who get involved in this kind of at-home business usually plant new crops of herbs (often started inside under grow lights from seed in small plastic flats) every two or three weeks in order to have a continuous supply during the growing season. The most popular herb is basil, used in pesto sauce for pasta and so good with tomatoes, but there are in fact several varieties of basil, and many herb growers plant two or three kinds. Fresh dill, chives, and tarragon are also good sellers. Specialized items such as lavender can also find a market in some areas. At-home herb growers usually don't bother with parsley since it is almost always available in supermarkets. Some raise less common varieties of mint, but one needs a lot of space for this herb and it must be kept off by itself so it doesn't take over the garden.

While this is usually a seasonal occupation, some people eventually put up a greenhouse to supply special customers, including restaurants, in winter.

Picnic Baskets

This is an idea that can bring in more money than you might think. In the Ozzie and Harriet days of yore, Harriet would have made the sandwiches and the potato salad and the brownies for the picnic basket. But these days Harriet is likely to work as long and hard at the office as Ozzie does, and a whole new group of service niches has appeared as a result.

In the major cities, upscale food shops do a thriving business in preparing picnic baskets, and the idea is catching on in smaller cities and suburban areas as well. In these harried times, a day's outing for a picnic is more of an "event" than it once was, whether the destination is the beach or a state or national park. Taking along a picnic basket stuffed with special treats, with no work involved excepting stopping on the way out of town to pick up the basket, makes for a much more delightful outing than stopping at some fast-food outlet along the highway.

People who succeed best at this kind of home-based food service offer menus that cover a broad range of tastes without listing so many dishes that preparation becomes unwieldy. For example, while potato salad and the cold eggplant dish ratatouille appeal to quite different palates, each can be paired with such different items as cold chicken, assorted sliced salami, or homemade country pâté for the sophisticated. If someone wants something special that isn't on your menu, such as shrimp salad, say yes but charge extra for it. Keep in mind that good bread, good cheese, and fresh ripe fruit cut across several categories of picnic. And be sure to offer a choice between a classy wicker basket and a plastic cooler for a returnable container.

Gift Baskets

You see them in every catalog of gourmet foodstuffs. They sit temptingly in the windows of upscale food shops. In fact, even the supermarkets carry them these days. Wicker baskets filled with goodies wrapped up in bright cellophane and decked out with ribbons and bows and plastic fruit are everywhere because they sell like mad. They're a useful gift for so many different occasions, and the perfect solution when you don't know what to give someone. With all those different things in them, there's bound to be something the person getting the basket will really like, and the rest may appeal to someone else in the family.

Of course, these gift baskets, even the supermarket versions, have prices on them that may cause some wonder. Can a straw basket and cellophane really increase the price of the edibles inside by *that* much? Well, no, if truth be told. This is a product with a huge markup. That means that there's room for you to go into the home-based gift-basket business and charge lower prices but still make hefty profits.

Whenever you see baskets of any shape or size on sale, grab them. The same goes for the gourmet goodies to go in them. But beyond keeping your costs down in this way, think about putting together humorous or offbeat baskets that contain even less expensive, but still fancily wrapped gifts. For example, one woman in this business picked up on the fact that elderly people, especially those who live alone, eat a great deal of canned soup. She started putting together very pretty baskets of wrapped-up cans of Campbell's soup, and they became a great success. Use your imagination!

Cooking Pamphlets

Are you the kind of cook who always has friends asking for your recipes? Well, it's very nice to give them to people, of course, but why not make some money from them? Putting together an entire cookbook is a major task, and usually requires that you have already established a reputation as a chef or teacher. Putting out a series of twenty-page pamphlets can not only help to build your reputation to the point that a cookbook publisher would be interested in doing a full-scale volume, but also earn you some very decent money along the way.

Personal computers have made desktop publishing so easy that thousands of individuals are putting out pamphlets of one kind or another every week. With the right software you can design a pamphlet on your PC that looks completely professional. Then take it to a local printer to run off whatever size printing you want, from one hundred copies to a thousand or more.

For recipe pamphlets, choose particular themes for each pamphlet, whether appetizers, desserts, or low-calorie main courses. Draw on your strengths. If you have particular knowledge of an ethnic cuisine, make the most of it. In the course of the last twenty years, America has gone from being a fairly provincial country in terms of what it would eat to one of the most avidly interested in the new and different.

Sell your pamphlets locally at gourmet food shops, kitchenware shops, and tourist boutiques. But it could also be worth your while to establish a home page on the Internet, which gives a couple of free recipes and offers your pamphlets by mail.

Knitting for Babies

Think small, and earn some large dividends. It is one of the ironies of life that babies, who hardly know or care what they are wearing, are always being given the cutest togs around. That includes a lot of hand-knitted goodies, from sweaters to caps and mittens, even diaper covers for special occasions. Few grandmas or aunts can resist the idea of giving their grandchild or niece or nephew a sweater or cap with the child's name inscribed on it. And of course, there are all those presents that have to be bought for baby showers even before the great event.

People who specialize in knitting for babies are on to a little psychological truth that makes this a surprisingly lucrative business: Even though a baby sweater takes much less time to knit than one for an adult, you don't have to scale your prices down accordingly. You can easily get away with charging a third of what you would for an adult sweater, even though the finished garment only took one fifth the time. People are astonishingly willing to shell out for baby clothes.

You can also increase your productivity by purchasing a knitting machine. These are small enough to be portable and fit easily on the kitchen table, and they still give a handmade look even as they speed up the process.

Bridesmaids' Dresses

The bride's wedding gown may come from the most expensive shop in town. Fine, she deserves it. But the bridesmaids' dresses are another matter entirely, and they can be a big problem. Some of the bridesmaids may have much tighter budgets than others, so the cost needs to be kept down even while satisfying the young women involved who are used to spending a lot on clothes. The color chosen and the cut of the dress should look nice on all the young women. Finally, at least some of the bridesmaids are likely to want a dress they can wear again.

In other words, successful bridesmaids' dresses need an expert eye and hand in charge. Do you have what it takes to become such an expert? If so, you can make very good money specializing in outfitting bridesmaids. You have to be a superior seamstress, of course, but you also need diplomacy, taste, and a talent for making women look elegant without breaking the bank. On the other hand, if you have those abilities, you can make excellent money in this specialized area. There's nothing like a wedding for generating word-of-mouth advertising for a job well done.

Costumes for Performing

Is there a ballet school in your community? How about a figure-skating club? A dinner theater or even a semiprofessional group that puts on several musicals a year? The young girls taking ballet classes are going to need tutus for recitals. The kids at the skating club, boys as well as girls, will require costumes for exhibitions and regional skating competitions. And that dinner theater will have a considerable costume budget, especially since theater-in-the-round dispenses with most scenery.

All of these performing activities mean potential customers for good seamstresses. If you can also design costumes, you have an opportunity to make considerable amounts of money. While costumes for young ballerinas tend to be fairly standard, and can even be passed down to younger children, and local theater costumes can often be recycled to a considerable extent in later productions, there are still a great many alterations to be made, which can bring in money even when you aren't starting from scratch.

But skating costumes are a particularly lucrative field that most people don't really think about. It is a general rule in the figure-skating world that each new competition program or exhibition routine must have a new costume. While figure-skating judges do not specifically give marks for costumes, competitors are fully aware that what they are wearing can sway a judge slightly for them or against them, and since competitions are often decided by as little as a tenth of a point (the margin by which Oksana Baiul beat Nancy Kerrigan for the Olympic Gold Medal), there is a lot of money to be made in figure-skating costumes.

Custom-Made Shirts for Men

Even top-quality brand-name dress shirts, costing sixty dollars and up, do not fit the bill for many men. Once the collar size gets above eighteen, for example, the major manufacturers, even the designer labels, assume that the arms should also be longer, or that there needs to be a good deal more cloth around the midriff. But human beings are not necessarily put together according to average measurements, and many men get sick of the search for something that will fit their own particular frame. I have a friend whose solution was to get his shirts custom-made in Hong Kong, where he sought out a tailor while on vacation. That's expensive, but not as exorbitant as the prices charged by some American companies that advertise in the back of national magazines.

There is a niche to be filled here, and if you can undercut those mail-order sources by a few dollars, and have the ability to turn out a beautifully made shirt, you can earn some very good money by developing a local clientele. An ad in the local paper will get you started, but if you know anyone who works at major companies in your area, have them spread the word at work about your shirts. You'll be astonished at the number of customers you'll get.

Tie-Dyeing

Tie-dyeing goes back thousands of years, when it was first practiced in the Orient. For some reason—perhaps simply because it was seen as different in America—the "flower children" of the 1960s took it up in a big way. It showed up on everything from T-shirts to jeans, becoming almost a uniform. Passing into the mainstream, it soon lost its cachet, and eventually became a joke.

But what goes around comes around. Tie-dyeing is back, in blazing colors. A recent fashion spread in *The New York Times* showed designer gowns accessorized with long tie-dyed scarves, and it is popping up all over the place. If you have a good sense of color, this is an easy way to get into the fashion business. A few boxes of dye, boiling water, and oversize rubber bands (for making the knots) are all you need to give T-shirts, white cotton trousers, or lengths of scarf cloth a new, vibrant life. Local boutiques can serve as an outlet, or you can set up at street fairs and flea markets. This can be an entertaining and creative way to earn some extra cash.

T-Shirts

Practically every mall in America has a T-shirt shop, but despite the seemingly wide variety of logos, they all end up having the same look—you instantly know where they came from. And if you want anything beyond basic lettering, prices can rise very fast. In fact, such shops have been a constant target of consumer watchdog groups. So these shops in no way have the market cornered.

Many people operate successful T-shirt businesses out of their own homes. They are prepared to run off a batch of shirts for a small local business or Little League team at good prices. They can make up special shirts for special occasions—birthdays, anniversaries, family reunions. A one-of-a-kind T-shirt is wanted as a gift? They can do it.

Because the mall T-shirt shops are so expensive, it is possible to undercut their prices with ease and still make a nice profit. And of course, a nice, original T-shirt is its own walking advertisement. "Where did you get that?" people want to know. And you've got another customer.

Embroidery

It used to be that everybody's aunt Tillie could do embroidery, and because Aunt Tillie and her ilk tended to embroider everything in sight, people got sick of the whole thing and began to roll their eyes at the mere mention of the word. As a result, embroidery became something of a lost art. When that occurs, the demand usually picks up again in time, and it's happening now. But because it is no longer a common skill, people who can do sophisticated and beautiful embroidery on pillows, linens, handkerchiefs, and napkins are much in demand.

Were you taught embroidery as a child and thought it was something you'd never do when you were an adult? Or did you take it up as a hobby after you were grown? (Some people have even started doing it as an aid to quitting smoking.) If it's a skill you possess, or want to learn, it can be much more than a hobby. Take out ads in local papers and you'll be astonished at the number of interested customers. Once you are well established, you may even find that a local boutique will be interested in having you do special-order work for it.

Since embroidery can take widely varying amounts of time to do, depending on the complexity and size of the job—from simple initials to an entire pillow—it is best to charge by the hour for such work.

Samplers

In the nineteenth century, virtually every home had a sampler displayed on the wall. These embroidered scenes, usually with a motto included, were the work of women of all ages from grandmothers to schoolgirls. They went out of fashion after World War I, and eventually enormous numbers of them were discarded. But fine examples are still found in museums and many private homes where antiques and family heirlooms are treasured.

Samplers are making a big comeback these days, along with many other arts and crafts from a century ago. But these days you don't see many insipid "Home Sweet Home" examples that once gave this art a bad name. Instead you will see extraordinary creations in vibrant colors and bold designs that can hold their own in a room full of modern abstract paintings. You will still see mottos or quotations embroidered on some of them, but they are very up-to-date, often funny quotes.

Anyone who has done macramé—which had a great vogue in the 1970s and early 1980s and is still fairly popular—can learn to do embroidery. And if you have the ability to make your own creations that go far beyond the kind of by-the-numbers macramé kits on sale, your embroidered scenes and designs, framed behind glass, can bring as good a price as many paintings or pottery bowls and vases made by local artists.

Quilt Making

Open just about any home-furnishing catalog and you will see quilts galore, on beds or used as throws on sofas or hanging on walls. Many of these are commercially manufactured, but handmade quilts have come roaring back into fashion, just as blown glass and handmade furniture have. In a world that is increasingly artificial, handmade crafts have become an antidote and are enjoying their greatest popularity since the nineteenth century. In hundreds of locales around the country, there are annual quilt festivals, where dozens of spectacular examples are displayed for sale and awarded prizes by a panel of judges.

Those who make quilts today have two advantages over the women who made them, often in groups at a quilting bee, in the previous century. The first advantage is vastly greater choice in fabrics, which can be bought cheaply at remnant stores. The second is the electric sewing machine. A beautifully hand-stitched quilt is still likely to carry off the blue ribbon at a judged exhibition, but it is perfectly acceptable these days to use a sewing machine, and the results can still fetch prices ranging from seventy-five to several hundred dollars, depending on the complexity and beauty of the finished product. The best of contemporary quilts are so in demand and so expensive that, as any antique dealer will tell you, the price of those made a century ago has plummeted in recent years. This is a craft revival from which real money can be made.

Making Curtains

Window curtains run the gamut from twenty-dollar-a-pair Wal-mart ready-mades to the thousand-dollar-a-window treatments created by top big-city decorators. There's no point in trying to make money at the low end—you can't compete with Southeast Asian factory products. And at the high end, top decorators have their own people to execute their elaborate creations. But there's plenty of room to make money in the middle. Many people with middle-management incomes are willing to spend three hundred dollars a window for a room or two in their homes. That price would include expensive fabric plus your work in making the curtains. If you have the sewing expertise to deal with pleats, swags, secure hook placement, and inner linings, there is a strong market for this kind of work.

At the beginning you will probably have to work independently, counting on ads and word of mouth to bring in customers, but as you become more established, it may be possible to develop a liaison with a fabric store in your area, with you and the store sending one another customers. Keep in mind that, like making wedding dresses or costumes, this is one line of work in which deadlines are particularly important. When people spend hundreds of dollars on new curtains, they usually have a party planned for a certain date to show off their newly decorated home, and your work *must* be completed on time.

Upholstering

There are people who do actual upholstering work in their homes—and they don't bother themselves with going to pick up the furniture, either. They do their work for stores that sell furniture—not large department stores, whose furniture lines are upholstered to order at the factories of the major manufacturers. Rather, they work for smaller, high-end furniture dealers who often give their customers the option of choosing fabric not available from the furniture manufacturer itself. Such jobs are often farmed out to small-scale upholstery experts who work in their own homes. The dealer brings the furniture and the fabric to the upholsterer.

This can be lucrative work, since customers who want such very specialized attention are perfectly willing to pay whatever they have to in order to get what they want. At the same time, you don't have to deal with the person who's actually buying the sofa or chair, but only with the furniture store that is using your services. Obviously this is not the kind of job for anyone without professional expertise, but many people who have had full-time jobs in this area find it a splendid way to keep on working after retirement. Many professions are difficult to pursue in one's later years, but upholsterers can go right on working at home at a less frantic pace, greatly supplementing their retirement benefits.

Furniture Slipcovers

It costs a fortune to have favorite sofas or easy chairs fully reupholstered, and slipcovers provide a sensible and far less costly alternative. The difficulty is that most commercially ready-made slipcovers are tacky, and often don't fit properly. This is a situation that provides opportunities for people with expertise in doing large-scale sewing jobs. You need to be good not only at precise fitting but also at making piping; however, the financial rewards are commensurate with the difficulty of the task.

It may often be possible for people to bring smaller chairs to your home and leave them with you, but with larger pieces this is one at-home job that may require going to other people's homes initially to take proper measurements. However, 90 percent of the work can be done at your home according to your own schedule. One of the reasons people who make slipcovers at home have a steady stream of customers is that it allows the owner of the chair or sofa to choose the fabric to be used. Since some fabrics are more difficult to work with than others, however, make it clear that a particularly heavy or patterned fabric that must be cut with special care will raise your price for the job.

Some people may want advice on fabric choice. Be firm about not going with customers to fabric stores, which can be very time-consuming, but be willing to give advice if they bring sample fabric swatches to you. This will also allow you to subtly steer customers away from fabrics that might be particularly troublesome to work with—not that you have to tell them that, of course.

Hand-Woven Rugs

There are few cheap good rugs anymore. As Third World countries improve their free-market standing and standard of living, the handmade rugs that it was possible to buy for a song twenty years ago have doubled and tripled in price. Sure, there are lots of inexpensive commercially made scatter rugs available, but they look like their price—cheap. But this has created an opening for hand-made rugs by American craftspeople, who were all but driven out of existence with the enormous growth in foreign imports that followed World War II. Like a lot of other American crafts, rug-making is burgeoning once again. Those who have training in this field, or have the aptitude and are willing to learn the craft, can make very good money on the side.

Braided and hooked rugs have come back into fashion, along with the hardwood floors that they look so good on. Wall-to-wall carpeting used to be the biggest boast going for rental units and even for new houses, but hard-wood floors are once again the essence of class, and they require rugs of all kinds and sizes. Hand-woven rugs in beautiful colors and patterns take time to make, but can command prices that undercut Oriental imports and still give those who create them a lucrative sideline—one that may even become full-time as the reputation of the crafts-person spreads. Those who get into this business usually find that they can charge a lot for rugs that are made to order in colors chosen by the customer.

Reweaving

Years ago, I witnessed a small tragedy. At a cocktail party, an older woman dropped her cigarette on her three-hundred-dollar white cashmere dress. The tears flowed. A few months later she showed up at another party in the same dress, minus the burn hole (and minus cigarettes), happy to tell the world that she had sent the dress to have the hole rewoven—and it had only cost fifty dollars!

There was a time when most good tailors could do reweaving, but it is now a specialty that is often done by people working out of their own homes. This kind of "invisible mending" is difficult, but anyone who has a gift for it can make substantial amounts of money. It is called for only when a very expensive dress or suit has been damaged, when people are willing to pay a hefty sum to save a garment that would require hundreds of dollars to replace. There is not a great deal of demand for this kind of work, but the fact that it is a rare skill that you charge a lot for more than makes up for intermittent call for your talents. In fact, that is one reason some people like doing it—the money is good without a large investment of time.

Small-Appliance Repair

The Smiths' Cuisinart died yesterday. Of course, they forgot to send in the warranty. Even if they had, who wants to box up a ten-pound machine and take it to the post office, and then wait weeks to get it back? If there were somebody who fixed such small appliances in the area, they'd take it over there in a minute. And that means that if you have the knack for making repairs to small appliances, there are plenty of customers to beat a path to your door.

In many cases, small appliances can be fixed with a minor rewiring job. If a part is needed, it can usually be obtained from the manufacturer; most are willing to ship out parts if you know exactly what is needed. But some people who do this kind of repair work make arrangements with local junk dealers and trash haulers, purchasing discarded machines and cannibalizing them for parts in good working order. Make clear to your customers what you are doing and give them a choice—if they'd rather pay the extra amount for an entirely new part, you can order it.

This kind of work is not for everyone, even among those able to do it. But if you're one of those people who enjoys tinkering with machinery anyway, it can be a nice source of extra income.

Car Repair

Are you one of those guys or gals (there are more women involved in this business than you might think) who can take an automobile engine apart and put it together again like a kid solving the puzzle of the Rubik's Cube while all the adults scratch their heads? Many people who are whizzes at automobile-engine repair learn to do it as a hobby when they're teenagers, but then go into some completely different line of work as adults. But if you have that kind of skill, why not make some side money with it by repairing cars in your spare time at home?

The number of car owners who have had unfortunate experiences getting their cars repaired at dealers or gas stations is astronomical. Many of them are more than willing to turn their car over to an independent repair person who's recommended by a friend. And if you are good at repair work, you will get talked about all over the place. Just a few satisfied customers and you'll have more work than you can handle. For that very reason, and to cut down on the need to send away for parts to many different manufacturers, most people who do this kind of work specialize in two or three makes of car. Some find it easier to concentrate on a commonplace, big-selling line, but others say they can make more money dealing with luxury imported models. Either way, if you are a born car tinkerer, you can make substantial money.

Lamp Rewiring

We live in a disposable age. Most people throw small appliances out if something goes wrong with them—and of course, many are made to go on the fritz as soon as the warranty expires. The same goes for lamps. The cord is worn, or the switch doesn't work properly? Throw the thing out and get a new one. Since that happens so often, people who do want to get a favorite lamp—or one that is a family heirloom—fixed often have a terrible time finding anyone willing to rewire it and install a new switch. The mom-and-pop businesses that used to do that kind of thing are fading away.

But while that kind of business may not get enough customers to pay the overhead of a commercial shop, there are enough to make this a good bet for making extra money at home. The investment in materials is small, and you don't need an electrician's license to do this kind of work, just basic electrical know-how. A small ad in the services section of a local newspaper will bring in customers. Once you're established, you won't even need to run an ad very often. This is the kind of work made for word-of-mouth advertising: "Oh, I know a gal who does that kind of work out on Willow Road."

You can charge fifteen to thirty dollars a lamp, depending on the complexity of the job, whether you have to buy a special switch, and whether it's a rush job. And customers whose antique lamps can now be turned on again at dusk in the front hall will be grateful ones.

Repairing China

This is an art. Taking a pitcher, decorative plate, or figurine that has fallen to the floor and broken into eight pieces and making it look almost new, with the break lines virtually invisible, requires a high degree of skill. People who can do this kind of work can add nicely to their income. Precious things get broken all the time, and if someone cherishes a piece enough to think of getting it repaired, he or she is more than willing to pay well to have it done. The object may not only be irreplaceable in that it isn't made anymore, but also have great sentimental value.

Those who do this kind of work have no trouble getting customers by placing the occasional ad and then relying on word of mouth. But they can also boost their income considerably by approaching local antique dealers. While something that has been broken will never fetch as high a price on the antique market as unblemished objects, some things are unusual enough to be worth repairing for sale, especially if they are part of a pair or set, and only a small piece has been broken off. Antique dealers are always on the lookout for people who can do this kind of work, so be sure to make your skills known to them.

Repairing Antique Clocks

Most contemporary clocks, even those that are encased in bodies that make them look like antiques, are run by quartz mechanisms or other computerized technology. That means that the real antiques, whether grandfather clocks with counterweight systems, or mantel clocks with elaborate wheels and gears, can be difficult to get repaired. To a large extent, old-school clock repairmen have gone the way of itinerant knife-grinders. But there are people who are fascinated by antique clock mechanisms, and love to work on them. Such people usually start out doing this kind of work as a hobby, but many of them come to the realization that they can turn that hobby into a moneymaking extra business.

The parts for many antique clocks simply are not made anymore. That means establishing contact with junk dealers or antique dealers who buy entire estates, and buying nonworking clocks from them for dirt-cheap prices simply to cannibalize the works for parts that may make it possible to repair a similar clock. Obviously this kind of work is only for the dedicated, but people who do it make very good money—getting that family heirloom to tick again is something people are willing to pay solid cash for. Because each job you undertake is an individual case, it is wise to get a good look at the problem and give the owner an estimate of the cost. An hourly labor fee, plus the cost of acquiring any parts, is the best way to go. Don't hesitate to charge twenty dollars or more an hour—this is specialized work with little competition.

Polishing and Refurbishing Metal

Many a blackened lamp, candlestick, or pot will, with sufficient elbow grease and the right cleaning products, reveal gleaming brass, shining silver, or glowing copper beneath decades of grime and soot. People have these objects in their cellars and attics, or may even buy them at flea markets because they like the shape. They plan to get to work one of these days and see what lies beneath the grime, but it is one of those jobs that most people keep putting off. Then they read your little ad in the back of the local paper, offering your services to make old metal look like new.

This is one of those odd services that wouldn't even occur to most people as existing, but that can bring a nice income when it is offered, suddenly inspiring people to root around in the cellar for that lamp that belonged to Grandmother and was too filthy to use but too interesting to throw away. And once the owner has it proudly displayed on a table, its story will get told to guests—who may well have a similar object they would like to see fixed up.

This at-home job can also blossom into a regular silver- or brass-polishing job for some customers. Once people recognize that they can trust you with their treasures, some will ask you if they can bring around their entire silver service for regular polishing. Your answer, of course, is, "By all means."

Refinishing Furniture

There are furniture-refinishing kits on the market today, and quite a lot of people buy them—and never get around to using them, or make a start and give up. This is not easy work, since it requires many steps, starting with the tiresome process of stripping the piece down to the original wood and then gradually building up the new finish. But some people truly enjoy doing it, and if you are one of them, there is very good money to be made plying this ancient trade in your extra time.

If you want to get into this business, start by refinishing some pieces of your own to show off to friends and neighbors. You'll get some work from them, and they will tell other people about your talents. It is not a bad idea at the beginning to have a matching pair of small end tables to show people, one in its original beat-up condition, the other restored to glowing beauty. This is one case in which a before-and-after comparison can speak volumes. Once you begin to advertise, it can be well worth the expense to have a small color brochure printed up with before-and-after photographs.

Some refinishing jobs can require additional skills. Veneer restoration, for example, requires a quite different set of skills. If you can do that kind of work, too, terrific, but don't undertake anything you're not certain you can carry out successfully. It's far better to tell a potential customer that something is beyond you than to botch the job. There's plenty of work out there even if you stick to straightforward refinishing.

Restoring Old Houses

I know a couple who, over the course of fifteen years, bought six different dilapidated but basically handsome houses in good areas, restored them while living in them for two or three years, then sold them at a huge profit and moved on to fix up another one. Both had full-time jobs and did the repair work in the evenings and on weekends. The seventh house they restored, they fell in love with and couldn't let go. But by that time they had earned more than seven hundred thousand dollars in clear profit, which they had invested in stocks and bonds. Both were able to take early retirement at the age of fifty-five.

This is far from an isolated example. Many people do this kind of work. It requires that between them, a couple have a broad range of skills, from carpentry to electrical wiring, so that contractors have to be brought in only for specialized jobs. They must also know the real estate market—the couple I described never used a real estate agent to sell a house, and the ones they bought, they usually acquired at auction.

Such work is only for the dedicated, but it can be extremely lucrative, and for those who enjoy fixing up old houses, it can be a pleasure as well.

Tutoring

Tutoring is the oldest teaching profession, predating not only public but private schools by hundreds of years. It was originally the means for teaching the children of emperors and kings, and until the twentieth century, remained largely an educational resource of the very wealthy. But these days hundreds of thousands of middle-class children are sent to tutors to get help in subjects they are weak in, or to prepare for college entrance exams.

The majority of tutors are either currently employed or retired teachers; it is a good way for substitute or part-time teachers to supplement their income. But a teacher's license is not a requirement. There are lab technicians who tutor kids in chemistry, writers who tutor pupils in English, and carpenters who give lessons in plane geometry. If there's a regular school subject at which you were always good, and if you have kept up with the field or are willing to spend some time perusing current textbooks, tutoring may be a good secondary job for you.

You need to be able to handle kids well, of course, and it helps to know how to tell parents diplomatically that their child has a serious problem in a subject or is simply not willing to pay attention and do the work. But even though you will run into some difficult cases, you will have many grateful thanks when your pupils pass that troublesome course or do well on an exam.

English-Language Tutoring for Immigrants

On July 5, 1997, *The New York Times* reported that the previous day more than five thousand people from 108 different countries took the oath of citizenship on Long Island. And this scene was repeated across the country. The level of immigration to the United States is a controversial issue these days, but America is a land of immigrants, and no one is seriously suggesting closing the door more than a little. In order to become citizens, immigrants must take a test that shows they are conversant with the English language and with the basic laws and history of their adopted land. That opens the door to another kind of at-home teaching.

Many immigrants who wish to become citizens enroll in special classes offered by educational and governmental institutions. But such classes are usually large, and there are always a considerable number of students who need or want more personalized attention. Anyone with a firm grasp of English as well as another language and a gift for communicating can do well tutoring immigrants. Some people specialize in one-on-one tutoring, but others find that having two or three students who speak the same foreign language can in fact speed things along. Some students may want fairly broad-based tutoring in English, while others just want to be able to pass the immigration test.

A background in some form of teaching can be helpful to do this kind of work for extra money, but it is not essential. The main thing that is needed, aside from fluency in English and another language, is patience.

Scholarship Consulting

The majority of young people who want to go on to college from high school these days need some kind of financial help. In the United States there are a vast number of different kinds of grants, scholarships, and loans available that go beyond those offered by individual colleges. They are offered by the federal government, by states, by educational foundations, and sometimes by wealthy private citizens. High school guidance or college admissions officers will know about some of them, but they have hundreds of students to deal with and may not even be aware of many kinds of available funds. That's where you come in, if you have a background in education or banking or state government. You're not going to get rich doing this kind of work (and many people who do it often offer their services virtually gratis to outstanding students from poor families). But these days even families with considerable income may need extra help in finding the necessary money to send a child to a first-rate college, and are willing to pay quite well for assistance. This kind of work is often done by recently retired people with some expertise in education or finance, who want to make a little extra money but who also want to keep their hand in and find this a particularly rewarding use of their time.

A fax and access to the Internet can be very important in doing this kind of work, helping you to get the latest information quickly; time is often of the essence for the students you will be trying to assist.

Teaching Computer Use

Many parents are feeling stupid these days because of their kids, who have learned in school, know how to use a computer when Mom and Dad don't. There are also a great many people over fifty who would like to learn to use a computer but are intimidated by them and don't want to invest in one unless they can first convince themselves that they will be able to make good use of it. Yes, there are plenty of large computer classes available, but a lot of people, especially older ones, don't want to embarrass themselves in the midst of a big group. Some libraries also offer basic instruction, but it often doesn't go far enough to make people really comfortable with computer use.

That's where you come in with one-on-one computer instruction that you provide in your own home. You'll need a professional-looking setup for this. People aren't going to feel comfortable at a computer station in the corner of your bedroom. But even a small extra room or a finished basement could provide the proper space. Obviously you need to be up-to-date on all the latest information on computer hardware and software. You don't need to own every specialized software program, of course, but you should be able to answer questions about it. That means reading the computer magazines and newspaper columns, but if you're interested in starting this kind of business, you undoubtedly do that anyway. One word of warning: Don't get into this kind of teaching unless you have lots of patience. Some clients are going to be very slow learners—which is, of course, why they need you in the first place.

Art Lessons

Have you been painting landscapes or still-life pictures for years on an amateur basis? Were you an art major (or minor) in college who went on to do something else instead? You can earn some extra money with your talent and expertise by giving painting lessons in your home. Yes, there are popular painting courses on cable television, but many amateur artists find these frustrating because the well-known teachers make things look easier than they actually are and because there's no one to ask questions of when a problem arises. And while many communities with a college or community college in the area have adult-education art classes available, there are many people who are too shy or insecure to attend them.

Giving private art lessons requires the teacher to adapt to the ability and the speed of learning of the student, of course. If you can't stand working with people who are all thumbs or whose taste is quite different from yours, then this isn't the kind of at-home job for you. Adult students can sometimes be more difficult to teach than children, who are more flexible and often more imaginative. Indeed, some private art teachers limit their teaching to kids for that very reason. There also can be an extra reward in teaching a child. Many people who give private art lessons have had youngsters start out with them and go on to become successful commercial artists, and occasionally noted serious artists. That possibility can give teacher as well as student a special sense of accomplishment.

Piano Lessons

As long as there are children, there will be a demand for piano lessons. Even in this age of synthesizers and other electronic gadgetry, when a parent senses that a child has some musical ability, the first thought that comes to mind is "piano lessons." Many kids who start with the piano go on to specialize in other instruments, string, brass, woodwind, or percussion. But the most common starting place is a seat at the piano. Even in very small towns, you can usually find at least one piano teacher.

As a piano teacher, you will sometimes have to deal with inept pupils and disgruntled parents who overestimated the ability of their offspring, but at the other end of the scale there will be some wonderful success stories and former students who will remember you with affection for the rest of their lives. When Cloris Leachman won the Best Supporting Actress Oscar for 1971's *The Last Picture Show*, one of the people she thanked for her success was her piano teacher of decades earlier!

Voice Lessons

Along with piano lessons, voice lessons are one of the mainstays of at-home moneymaking. A great many people with serious musical training and even considerable professional experience eventually turn away from the uncertainties of a professional singing career, but thousands of them continue to exploit their experience by becoming part- or full-time voice teachers. I've known voice teachers who ranged from a woman who had been a nightclub star in Chicago—and gave Liberace his first job as an accompanist when he was nineteen—to a woman who played leads in college musicals but went on to become a psychologist.

Most vocal teachers give individual lessons, but many arrange to have group sessions once every couple of months when students get to perform songs they have been working on in front of one another. A great many voice teachers specialize in working with children—think of those thousands of little girls who have auditioned for productions of *Annie,* or who regularly compete in juvenile beauty contests. They all have voice teachers.

Being a voice teacher means doing your best and being diplomatic with students who have a minimum of natural talent, which means you have to have patience, but you are also bound to have some students who will make you proud down the line. The going rates for voice teachers these days range from fifteen dollars per hour and up, depending upon locale and the level of instruction being given.

Baton-Twirling Lessons

In this era of computer games and in-line skates, you would think that an old-fashioned skill like baton twirling would have been left behind. But as televised holiday parades and a visit to any high school football match indicate, this is still a very popular talent. At the Macy's Thanksgiving Parade, in between the floats and high-flying giant balloons, there are always high school bands from across America, with fresh-faced girls twirling their batons and flinging them into the air before catching them again.

Did they teach themselves all these tricks? Certainly not. And while many high schools have a female teacher or coach on staff who instructs the girls in baton twirling, a great many parents see to it that their daughters get private lessons as well. As the infamous "high school cheerleader murder plot" in Texas a few years ago shows, the competition among cheerleaders is fierce. Many girls want or need extra lessons.

Any woman who was an experienced baton twirler in her youth—like bicycle riding, it is said that the skill is never forgotten—could make extra money giving lessons in her backyard. An ad in the local paper, or even just a notice on school bulletin boards, is bound to bring in customers. One of your students could end up in the Macy's parade or displaying her skill in a beauty pageant. (At least one Miss America had baton twirling as her skill, as have several runners-up.) You can certainly charge ten dollars an hour for such lessons. Just don't get involved in any murder plots.

Make Your Garden Grow and Pay

A woman in Lititz, Pennsylvania, had a garden that was the envy of her neighbors and friends, which she was proud to open to the public on annual garden-tour weekends. She was constantly being asked for advice on when to divide hosta plants, or how to combat Japanese beetles. She sometimes muttered to herself about all the free advice she was passing out—and got an idea. For the past several years, for three weekends in the spring, three in August, and three in the fall, she has given gardening lessons in her own backyard.

Her fence-enclosed garden is not large by some standards—only eighty by thirty feet—but she found she could accommodate a dozen students at once, instructing them as she put in her usual complement of new annuals in the spring and midsummer, showing when to cut back perennials and how to put the garden to bed for the winter. This was all work she would have done anyway, but she found that many beginning gardeners, men as well as women, were willing to pay thirty-five dollars apiece to watch her work. At the end of each session, she serves light refreshments. People have come to her sessions from many surrounding towns, and about half keep coming year after year since she always puts in some different plants. Even with the modest amount she expends on refreshments subtracted, she earns about thirty-five hundred dollars in extra money each year. That pays her longtime gardening expenses of about one thousand dollars a year and gives her a twenty-five-hundred-dollar profit as well.

Teaching Bridge

The game of bridge is the most complex of the popular card games. People can pick up the rules to poker or even canasta quite quickly, but the bidding system on which bridge is based scares off a great many people. Yet people who like to play bridge tend to be fanatical about it. Many a budding romantic relationship or new marriage can run into trouble if one partner is a terrific bridge player and the other is reluctant to learn.

That's where you come in. If you are a whiz at bridge, hold classes in your home for bridge novices. Since everyone but you will be a beginner, your students can feel more relaxed about learning the intricacies of the game and less fearful of making mistakes. What's more, they won't have to be embarrassed in front of the spouse or romantic interest who has been urging them to learn the game. Keep your classes small, with only one or two foursomes playing at once, so that you can give everyone special attention. Even charging as little as fifteen dollars per lesson, two tables of players per week can bring in some nice extra cash.

Cooking Lessons

Are your dinner parties the envy of your friends and neighbors? Do you have a knack for showing other people how to do things? Do you have an extremely well equipped kitchen, with plenty of room to move around? Then perhaps you should consider giving cooking lessons. Major cities have famous—and very expensive—cooking schools. But in smaller cities, towns, and suburbs, there is much less likelihood that you will be competing with a famous chef or brand-name cooking school.

Statistics show that more Americans are eating out than ever before, and doing it more frequently. But there is another side to this coin. There are also more food magazines than there have ever been, more cooking contests, and a greater interest than ever in the cuisines of foreign countries. Thus, while those who don't like to cook—or are leading the kind of "rat race" lives that leave them no time for it—are flocking to restaurants, those who like to cook are more intensely interested than ever before. That means that you can attract a lot of students.

The ability to teach the cuisines of other countries around the world is in particular demand. Were your parents immigrants, so that you have a good knowledge of the food of their country of origin? Or are you an immigrant yourself, with a good command of English? Perhaps you come from old American stock but have spent some time living in a foreign country. Make some money with your talent and expertise. Be sure to keep class sizes small enough so that your kitchen doesn't get too crowded— even if that means only two students at a time. At twenty-five to thirty-five dollars a session, you can still make plenty of extra money.

Teaching Signing

It used to be that the majority of the population regarded signing by the deaf as something strange and unsettling. But all that has changed. When Louise Fletcher won the Oscar for Best Actress for her performance in *One Flew Over the Cuckoo's Nest* in 1976, millions of people were touched by the way she signed her acceptance speech to her deaf parents. A new attitude was born, and interest in signing grew steadily, topped off when the lovely deaf actress Marlee Matlin won the Best Actress Oscar for *Children of a Lesser God* ten years later, just as her Broadway predecessor, Phyllis Frelich, won the Tony Award for the original play.

Over the past two decades, the National Theater of the Deaf has had enormous success across the country, and special signed performances of regular plays and even operas are regularly presented. There are now a great many hearing people who have become fascinated with the art of signing. If you are fluent in this beautiful and astonishing form of communication, you can certainly make money teaching it to others. It can be taught at home in the evenings to individual pupils or small groups. Your fees should be similar to those charged by music teachers in your area.

Lamaze Training

There are many group classes for the Lamaze Method of giving birth available across the country. But not everyone interested in this popular technique feels comfortable about group classes. Many parents-to-be would be happier in a private setting—for some women, this may be the key to securing the participation of their husbands.

If you are a registered nurse with experience in the Lamaze Method, giving private instruction in your home could be an excellent way to extend your income. Be sure to contact local physicians who are open to the Lamaze Method (not all are in favor of it), to let them know about your instruction sessions. Referrals from doctors can be as important as word of mouth in pursuing this kind of extra work.

Travel Agent

This is a favorite at-home job for many people who have previously worked in airline reservations or at a regular travel agency. Other people take advantage of mail-order training organizations, but with these you must be careful to check out the offer thoroughly—there are some rip-off companies in this business. It is, of course, essential to have a computer, fax, and answering machine to do this kind of business. But if the start-up costs can be relatively high, so can the rewards.

Quite aside from the commissions you take in from airlines, cruise-ship companies, and hotels, travel agents are given a large number of opportunities to travel themselves at minimal cost. In fact, many people who do this kind of work have taken it up primarily because they like to travel, and such a job makes it possible for them to do it much more often and much more glamorously than would otherwise be the case.

Before you take any steps to set up such a business, however, be certain to check out the zoning regulations and other restrictions that may apply in your locality. In some residential areas, for example, there can be laws that forbid putting out an office sign. I know a woman who has a home-based travel business despite this particular restriction, which she gets around by having a very noticeable oil painting of a tropical scene on an easel in her front window. This won't work to bring in passersby, which she doesn't want anyway, but helps first-time customers whom she has talked to on the phone find her easily.

Preparing Income Tax Forms

Yes, there are nationally advertised income tax preparation firms that operate all across the country. They're fine for people who don't have terribly complicated financial situations but are befuddled even by fairly simple forms (as they have every right to be when it comes to the output of the Internal Revenue Service). And the wealthy usually have personal accountants who take care of tax forms as well as providing many other services. But that still leaves a lot of people with moderate incomes but fairly complicated tax situations. That includes freelancers of almost any kind, people who run one-person businesses, and people who make extra income operating out of their homes—many of the very people this book is about.

If you're good at bureaucratic paperwork and math (even with computers, you need to be sufficiently well versed in mathematics so that you *could* do the work without a computer), this may be an excellent secondary job for you. It means keeping up with all the latest tax provisions, federal, state, and local (and some of them will change every year). An instinctive grasp of what will look fishy on a tax return and what will sail by is a big advantage. And because this work is mostly seasonal, crammed into the months of February, March, and April, you must be prepared to work long hours when the crunch is on. But you can make a lot of money in that period. Some people who do this work charge by the hour, others according to the number and kind of forms they are dealing with for each client. Clients will be willing to pay at least twenty-five dollars an hour for this kind of work.

Freelance Bookkeeping

Freelance bookkeeping as a side job has always existed. But with the hectic pace of our contemporary world, and the proliferation of two-job families, there is a greater need for it than ever. What's more, with the personal computer revolution and the development of sophisticated spreadsheet software, it has become easier than ever to set oneself up in this kind of side business. You don't necessarily have to be a certified public accountant (although that will often make it possible to charge higher prices). An ad in the local paper will bring you plenty of customers who are too busy to do their own accounting, or feel incapable of doing a good enough job.

Although this is a year-round at-home job, you can expect extra customers when the post-Christmas bills come in and at tax time. At such times it is better to turn away customers than to shortchange your regulars. Plan to charge by the hour—twelve dollars and up is reasonable, depending on the area you live in. You will undoubtedly find that some of your customers are people who, like you, have their own home businesses, but in other areas, and who need help keeping track of their accounts.

Typing/Word Processing

Computers were supposed to create something called "the paperless office." But as many news reports have pointed out, the opposite has happened, There's more paper floating around offices and businesses and college campuses than ever before. Yet, in the age of "downsizing," there are often fewer people to do the work of churning out reports on computers. In major cities, there are many people who make their living doing this kind of work for businesses in the midnight hours when the offices are otherwise closed. And there's still work that gets farmed out to freelancers who work at home.

If your typing skills are first-rate and you own a personal computer, there is very good money to be earned typing up and printing out all kinds of reports at home. If you're good, firms will be perfectly happy to send the work over to you by messenger, and it's often possible to get fifteen to twenty-five dollars an hour depending on where you live and the nature of the work.

Internet Researcher

Although we read constantly about the coming Information Age, in which almost everyone—at least in First World countries—will be linked by computers, the Internet, and other communications wonders, we aren't there yet. Less than 40 percent of homes have personal computers, and despite all the hoopla about the Internet, only about 27 percent of PC users were linked to it by the fall of 1997. That opens the way for individuals with a PC and Internet access, plus a good knowledge of what is on the Internet and how to track it down quickly, to make some money.

Although the Internet is still in its infancy, there is already a great deal of information available on it, as well as a vast amount of junk information, misinformation, and outright falsehoods. Many people would like to be able to get hold of some of the good information on the Internet, but don't have a computer or the time and expertise to surf the Internet successfully. That provides a possible form of at-home work. Instead of simply exploring the Internet for your own entertainment, you could provide a service for people who haven't yet joined the computer parade by finding information for them, printing it out, and handing it over to them.

There are already people doing this kind of work with great success. They charge the same kinds of fees that any other researcher would (twelve dollars and up per hour, depending on where they live and their level of expertise), plus any charges incurred for the retrieval of information that isn't free. Click on and make some money.

Word Doctor

Do you have first-class writing and editing skills? Many people do not, including numerous people with good college degrees, sometimes even advanced degrees. There are lots of professional people who are called on from time to time to make a speech, draft a committee report, or who have an idea they would like to express in a publishable article. They can often write a perfectly acceptable sentence, but may have a problem putting a series of sentences together into a cogent paragraph. Or they may be able to write a fine paragraph, but have trouble making the transition from one paragraph to another, giving their speech or report a herky-jerky quality. Others may have a problem with organization, so that the real beginning of the piece is found lurking several pages into it. And some people just write prose that, while perfectly correct, is so dull it would put a hyperactive child to sleep.

Such people need help. If you can smooth out their prose, show them how to reorganize it, and give it some pep, you can make excellent money fixing up their work. A small ad in the local paper will bring you surprising clients—doctors, lawyers, ministers, as well as the more expected businessmen. Charge by the hour, and don't undersell yourself. The price you charge will depend on the size of the community, but even in a small city you shouldn't hesitate to ask twenty dollars an hour. If people say that's a lot of money, make clear that you are offering a professional service, and that in a major city they could expect to pay twice as much. Always get a partial advance, and don't get involved if people want you to do a job—a magazine article, say—for nothing, but will pay you when it gets published.

Speech Coach

Do you know how to give a good speech? Have you a background in acting or teaching? Then you may be able to make some very good extra money by helping professional people to give good speeches. This is likely to require some writing or editing skills as well as a knowledge of how to present oneself in front of a group. The main problem some of your clients will have is that their speeches are dull or confused, and they will need your assistance in the composition of the speech itself. But other people may be perfectly capable of writing a good speech, yet have great difficulty in delivering it well. They will need coaching in how to stand in front of a group, how to pace the speech so that it is neither too slow nor too fast, and how to accentuate words to give their delivery some pep. There are people who don't speak loudly enough or who don't enunciate clearly, and they will need vocal coaching to overcome those problems.

Some professionals are simply terrified of giving a speech, and will need a program of training that helps them overcome their fears. This writer knows a woman who started out coaching people in her home, then wrote a book on the subject, and now gives seminars in rented hotel conference rooms for several hundred dollars for a two-day course, and has been hired by many corporations to train their executives.

Party Planner

We live in a time when an enormous number of people eat out most of the time, and buy takeout when they eat it. Not only are their culinary skills deficient, they wouldn't even know how to begin to plan a party to be given in their own homes. But the time will come when they have to do it, either for a special occasion that demands at-home entertaining, or in order to repay friends for all those parties they've gone to at other people's houses.

A party planner doesn't have to provide the food or do any of the actual work. He or she simply offers a service that arranges for all of the work to be done. The party planner advises on everything from the kind of invitation that is appropriate, to the sort of party that will best serve the needs and budget of the hosts. The party planner goes over the menu possibilities, whether for a cocktail party, a buffet, or a sit-down dinner, and then deals with the caterer, hires the bartender, and looks after every detail. The hosts don't have to do a thing but pay the people you hire—and you, for your expert advice.

If you know how to give a great party yourself, and have a congenial personality but still know how to be firm—with your clients as well as with the caterer you hire for them—you can make a very nice income at this kind of work, most of which you can do from your own home office, aside from meeting with your clients at their homes or apartments to get the lay of the land. What you really are is a *facilitator*—a new kind of "middleman" for our complex and fast-paced times.

Calligraphy

Beautiful handwriting is a rarity these days. Most of us don't worry much about our illegible scrawls and scratchings. But we do wonder, when we see beautiful handwritten script on a wedding invitation or place card at a dinner party, who in the world did that. In most cases, if we know the bride or hostess, we can be quite certain that she didn't execute those perfect curlicues.

Some people have a natural gift for handwriting—which, when it is good enough and has a consistent style, rises to the level where it can be called calligraphy, the art practiced by monks in the Middle Ages and the Renaissance. There are numerous books that illustrate various styles of calligraphy, from the simple but elegant to the truly ornate. If you have an ability to do this kind of work, there is nice quiet money to be made writing the names on wedding invitation envelopes and place cards. While it is true that there are now computer software programs that make it possible to print out words in a calligraphic style, that's still not the same thing as handwritten versions, which radiate class. The occasional ad in the local paper, plus word of mouth, can bring you a steady stream of customers. Be sure to make yourself known to local stores that have wedding-present registries; leave samples of your work with them, since they are likely to be asked on occasion if they know anyone who does calligraphy. And you may eventually get some major jobs such as writing menus for dinner parties or even restaurants.

Flower Arranging

Of course, there are florists galore in the yellow pages. But the bouquets from florists tend to have a studied sameness about them—and that's not just the wire-service bouquets, either. Yes, there are elite florists who do spectacular things in major cities, but they charge amounts that can add several thousand dollars to the cost of a major party or wedding. There is an in-between niche in flower arranging, and many people make a lot of money filling it, operating out of their own homes.

What these people excel at is providing flower arrangements that seem special, even unique, without costing the equivalent of a week's wages. Start small, doing arrangements for the parties of friends. Then take out an ad. Word of mouth will do the rest. Some people in this business eventually branch out, hiring extra help, but most remain one-person operations, doing the arrangements for smaller parties of all kinds.

Framing Pictures

Yes, there are frames on sale everywhere, and most locales have shops that specialize in framing pictures that don't fit the standard measurements sold in most stores. But those who have special pictures to be framed, of an unusual size or value that demands special treatment, are often shocked at the prices charged by frame stores. But one reason their prices are so high is the rent they must pay on central locations in the same area as high-priced boutiques and antique shops. If you have the talent for mat-cutting and woodworking necessary to do the job, you can undercut the prices charged by the frame shops by working out of your home in your spare time.

This is a good way for people with well-equipped home woodworking shops to make all that expensive equipment pay for itself. Some of those who take up framing on this professional basis also cut their own glass, but a deal can usually be worked out with your local glazier if you prefer to work that way. It's really not worth going into this side business to do ordinary framing jobs, but if you have the ability to promote yourself as a specialist in high-end work, you can make a lot of extra cash while still giving your customers the feeling that they've gotten their money's worth.

Photo Albums

Many people take photos of their vacation trips or of family occasions and then stick them away in a drawer or a box, saying that one of these days they'll put them together into some nice albums. But then they never quite get around to doing it, and feel a twinge of guilt every time they open that drawer or look at that box on the closet shelf.

That provides an opening for clever people to start a small side business organizing people's photos for them in attractively put together albums. Have your customers bring in their piles of photos and spend an hour going through them, so that you know the names of the people and places in the pictures. Then you do the arranging and mounting, whether in a simple, straightforward way or preparing an elaborate album with stickers or small drawings to decorate the pages. Offer a range of different album sizes and covers, as well as the use of different mounting techniques, from glueing the photos in to mounting them in photo corners or encasing them in clear plastic.

This is a slightly tricky business to get started, because people may not quite understand what's involved from a small ad. It can be more helpful to put together some sample albums for good friends for free with the understanding that they'll show them to other people and send some business your way. Once you've gotten a few actual customers, however, the clients will come in a steady stream. Keep in mind that some of your customers are likely to be older teenagers who've grown up enough to realize that a surprise album of this kind can be a great birthday gift for parents. Kids who are about to go away to college may find this a particularly neat idea.

Hairstylist

Home beauty parlors are an American tradition. You can find them everywhere, from small towns to the side streets of major cities, even New York. They charge less than a full-scale beauty salon that employs several people, but that's not the reason most people go to them. The success of the home beauty parlor usually has as much to do with the gregarious, kind, and funny proprietor. For many women, their favorite hairstylist serves much the same purpose as a favorite bartender does for men: someone to talk to about life's big and little problems. But for women, instead of getting drunk in the process of unloading their problems, they come out looking prettier.

A home beauty parlor requires a substantial initial investment in equipment and plumbing, but it can pay off nicely over the long run. Many of those who establish a home beauty parlor start by opening three nights a week, usually Wednesday, Thursday, and Friday, and all day Saturday. They often plan to do this kind of work full-time down the line, but are smart enough to get a customer base firmly established before quitting their regular jobs.

Wig Styling

After Betty Furness stopped opening refrigerator doors for Westinghouse in television ads, she became a consumer affairs advocate, first for New York State and then for New York City. When she was interviewed about her new role on the "Tonight Show," Johnny Carson complimented her on her hair. She announced it was a wig—becoming the first prominent woman to make such an admission—and wigs were suddenly back in style. The late Eva Gabor made a fortune out of her wig business (more than she ever made as an actress). Younger women wear wigs the way their grandmothers wore hats, to dress themselves up, while many older women need wigs because of thinning hair. Others simply find them convenient.

But a good wig needs constant care, and many women don't have the time or talent to attend to them properly. A wig stylist working at home can make good money taking on this task, without the large investment in equipment that's necessary to open a regular beauty parlor. Some women who were trained as beauticians but can't stand the endless chitchat involved in running a beauty parlor (the *Steel Magnolias* ambiance is not for them) find that wig styling is the perfect way to make use of their training in peace and quiet.

Makeup Specialist

There are women, whether plain or beautiful, who have a knack for applying makeup. They always look great. But there are a very large number of women—sometimes

even very beautiful women—who just don't seem to be
able to get it right. The lipstick and eye shadow are in
clashing colors, or too heavily applied, and the result is
that they magnify their facial faults while obscuring the
elements that should be emphasized.

If you have a gift for makeup, start a spare-time business doing makeup for special occasions and teaching
your clients how to do better by themselves. When a
woman who has always looked dowdy or vulgar because
of her lack of talent in doing her own makeup suddenly
shows up looking terrific, people really take notice. That
is great advertising for you. As time goes on, makeup
specialists often find that their expertise is in demand for
larger projects—doing the makeup for the community theater group, or assisting the members of entire wedding
parties.

For individual jobs, it's best to charge by the session
for this kind of work, even though some may take a little
longer than others. For larger groups such as wedding
parties, set a price that covers everyone, even though
some people will need your help less than others.

Nail Care

Why would anyone come to your house for a manicure
when she can get it done at the beauty parlor while having her hair done? Because people are extremely fussy.
Many women find the perfect hairstylist for themselves,
but just don't like the resident manicurist at that beauty
salon for one reason or another. They're perfectly willing
to make an extra stop (at your house) to get their nails
done to their liking. What's more, in the last decade there
has been a tremendous increase in the number of men

who have their nails professionally manicured. But there are many men who want beautifully kept nails yet are not happy with having them done in public in a unisex salon. Maybe they're being silly, but it makes more customers for your home-based service.

Specializing in nail care will bring in extra income without the expense of investing in the plumbing and machinery necessary to run a home-based beauty salon. It's a small, quiet business that is built on your superior skill.

Personal Trainer

The fitness craze has been going on for many years in America, and shows no signs of abating. But Americans are also somewhat schizoid about physical fitness—in 1996 the sales of high-fat premium ice cream took a big jump upward, while low-fat versions decreased. This just means more work for those who want to stay trim, and more customers for people who become personal trainers.

Yes, there are plenty of gyms for people to go to, and the very wealthy indulge themselves with personal trainers who come to their homes. But some people, especially women, do not like gyms or working out with strangers in a group, and personal trainers who make house calls charge the earth. There is room in between for the personal trainer who has customers come to his or her home for private, individualized sessions.

You will, of course, need to have workout equipment, which means a capital investment, although most people who go into business as personal trainers have already purchased such equipment for themselves. It's wise to have a room set aside for the workout sessions—a finished basement is fine. And there should be a nicely appointed adjacent bathroom where the client can shower afterward. While your basic costs may be more than for some at-home jobs, setting up as a personal trainer can also be a very lucrative field.

Preparing Astrological Charts

I have a friend who took a lower-level employee who had been extremely helpful out to lunch as a way of saying thank you. They went to an Italian restaurant, where the host crunched into some broken glass in his *pasta e fagioli* soup. When he got home, he looked up his horoscope. It said, "This is a bad day to repay a debt. Don't bite off more than you can chew." It is incidents of this kind that cause vast numbers of people to take astrology at least somewhat seriously; many people take it very seriously.

If you have a genuine interest in astrology, to the point that you have learned how to do charts for your friends, consider actually going into business in this field. People who take astrology seriously are willing to pay $35 to $150 to have their charts done, the price varying with the complexity and depth of the chart requested. There is a great deal of reference literature on this subject, which can be extremely useful, but these days many people who do astrological charts as a moneymaking sideline put a great deal of information on a home computer. This takes a lot of work initially, but will pay off when you get to the point that you need only to punch a few keys to get a fundamental readout for any day in the past twenty-five to fifty years.

While a small ad in the local paper will bring you customers, this is one case in which a slightly larger ad specifically placed on the newspaper page where the daily horoscope appears can pay extra dividends.

Tarot Readings

You do not have to wear a turban, festoon yourself with ten pounds of junk jewelry, or buy a crystal ball to give tarot readings. Nor do you have to rig up tables so they move at the right moment, have a tape playing weird sounds that seem to come from the ceiling, or try to contact the dead. While some people who do crystal-ball readings or hold séances also read tarot cards, the tarot has a long history with precise, specified interpretations. It's not a matter of fakery, but of shuffling and dealing out a tarot deck in the prescribed manner and reciting from memory the meanings that are associated with each card, according to the order in which that card appears.

There are a great many different tarot decks that you can buy. They are almost always beautiful—many major artists have created designs for tarot decks, from the unknown master who created the famous Visconti deck during the Renaissance, to Salvador Dalí. Over the centuries, many famous decks have been created, with varying interpretations, but each deck has its own specific meanings for each card. In recent years, several New Age decks have been created. But most decks use the same basic system of laying out the cards, and the interpretations of each card vary more in style than in basic substance.

Those who do tarot readings generally offer a selection of decks to the customer, who is likely to make a choice based on which has the designs that are most pleasing to him or her. A reading can easily be completed in half an hour, and readers generally charge from twenty to thirty dollars. That may seem high, but in this instance a lower price would be counterproductive—the customer expects to pay for a special experience.

Wake-Up Calls

A woman in St. Louis has an unusual service that could do well in any city. She makes wake-up calls to customers who have an early plane to catch, a business breakfast, or need to get on the road at an ungodly hour. Her clientele is made up of single men and women in their twenties and early thirties who work hard and play hard and have a tendency to reach over and turn off the alarm clock repeatedly, or who are simply worrywarts about not making appointments on time. She grew up on a farm and has never managed to shake the habit of waking at dawn, but now earns some extra money out of the fact that she's up before anyone else.

Although her primary business is wake-up calls, she also has a few clients who give her the additional job of serving as a reminder service. If all this sounds like the Broadway musical and subsequent movie starring Judy Holliday, *Bells Are Ringing*, our St. Louis friend is well aware of it. She named her service HI-aleha, in keeping with the racetrack betting operation that was going on without Judy Holliday's knowledge in the movie. Sometimes her clients even have her call up friends to sing "Happy Birthday."

Two kinds of payment schedules are offered. There's a flat monthly rate (which, it's made clear, will go up for more than forty calls a month) and a per-call rate that's preferred by people who use the service only occasionally.

The flat rate is fifty dollars a month, while the per-call rate is two dollars each time.

Taping TV Shows

In a 1997 poll, Americans rated the VCR their favorite invention of the second half of the twentieth century. But industry estimates make clear that more than half of those who own VCRs don't really know how to use them. They can pop in a videotape that they've rented or bought, but can't deal with programming the VCR to tape a show on television that they'd like to be able to see again or that they aren't able to take the time to watch when it is first broadcast. Even with the advent of the VCR Plus system, which allows viewers to simply punch in the numbers following each show in a local television guide, many people are nervous about it, or simply forget to do it time after time.

That's where you come in. Record programs for other people on request at your own home. You will need to have two or three television sets and VCRs in order to accommodate customers who want recordings of separate programs that air at the same hour. Be prepared to record anything from soap operas to the Super Bowl. If you supply the blank tapes, you may be able to get them wholesale, and add some more to your income that way. Have a set fee for half-hour, hour, and two-hour programs, with even higher fees for miniseries and open-ended events such as sports or award shows.

All of this is perfectly legal. You are not recording programs for resale but simply providing a service for people who want specific programs recorded for their own use.

Home-Cleaning Service

No, this is not a matter of charging out the front door and personally cleaning other people's homes or apartments. Rather, you hire and train a small staff to do the cleaning. Some of your employees may only want to do this part-time, and working through you can give them greater flexibility than they would find with a large employment agency. And since you're not just a middleman, like the big agencies, you can be choosier and keep a better eye on your small staff. You'll also know what kinds of tasks your employees are particularly good at—the person who is good at basic cleaning may not be the best choice for a major clean-out-the-closets job.

If you live in an area where there are one or more colleges, you will probably find plenty of students who are willing to do this kind of work, and can be fairly sure they'll be polite and congenial on the job. Even so, it is a good idea to bond your employees. This not only takes care of the problem in the unhappy event that a client finds something missing, but also gives your clients a greater sense of confidence. You certainly won't have any trouble finding customers in this age of two-income families. Many people simply don't have the time to do household cleaning these days.

In running this kind of business, all money passes through you. Your clients pay you by check, and you pay your employees.

Take in Ironing

The very word *ironing* causes a lot of people to clutch their foreheads and moan. But there are in fact people who actually enjoy doing it, and if you are one of those, you can make some nice money catering to the needs of people to whom the word is anathema. Even in this age of permanent press, there are clothes that need to be pressed, or embroidered pillowcases that really should be ironed when weekend guests are coming. Sure, there are commercial cleaning establishments that will take care of the job, but the results often leave something to be desired, and the fresh smell of clean laundry seems to have been replaced by an unpleasant chemical odor.

There are people who have the money to get things properly ironed and who are willing to pay a premium to have them done right on an individual basis. You will no doubt find that some people will beg you to come do the ironing at their homes or apartments. Just say no, politely but firmly. If they want it done, they bring it to you. Charge by the hour, and don't hesitate to ask at least double the minimum wage—this isn't old-fashioned maid's work in this day and age but a luxury service.

Car Washing and Polishing

There are those who take great pleasure in washing and polishing their own cars, spending whole Saturday afternoons doing a loving job. But most people don't have the time for that, and a lot of people hate it. They opt for the commercial drive-through car wash. Such establishments make a car look presentable, but not much more. And for a surprising number of people, that really isn't enough. Americans are proud of their cars. Many are status symbols of a high order, and a status symbol that looks less than its best loses its impact.

All over the country there are people who wash cars in

their own driveways for paying customers, giving them the kind of careful washing that they never get at a commercial car wash, and then hand-polishing them so they glisten like jewels in the sun. They also deal with more difficult jobs such as vinyl tops and convertibles in a customized way. An interior vacuuming job finishes things off.

This isn't an at-home job that can be done in a neighborhood where the houses are close together and the driveways short. The neighbors won't like it. But if you have the space, it can be a well-paid extra job. Many people are willing to pay as much as thirty-five dollars for a superior job, and by doing several cars a weekend, you can tote up a nice extra income.

Resume Rewrites

Young people about to graduate from college, older workers who want to change professions or who have been downsized after years with the same company, people returning to the job market after a hiatus, all have one thing in common: they need a good resume. Sure, there are books on the subject. But because everyone's experience is different from everyone else's, it's perfectly possible to read such a book and still leave out something you should have put in, or put something in you should have left out. Personal consultation with an expert on resumes can make a big difference in getting a job quickly.

If you have expertise in this area, there is good money to be made. You can easily charge seventy-five dollars a resume, even more if you also do the final version on your own PC, giving it a really professional look. Different fields require somewhat different approaches in terms of resumes, so you do have to know your stuff. You also need to have a gift for drawing people out, getting them to tell you enough about themselves so that their skills, knowledge, and personal qualities can be presented in the best possible light. There's a considerable degree of psychology involved in putting together a good resume, which also makes it interesting work.

Some people who rewrite resumes also offer advice on how to make a good impression in an interview, which doubles the fee they can charge. If you have a background in personnel work, this may be just the right at-home job for you.

Term-Paper Writing

The mother of a college friend of mine made her living by writing term papers for students. Well, there are worse ways of making an illegal living. But let's be clear about this. Students who turn in other people's work as their own are guilty of plagiarism, and they can be put on probation or even expelled for doing it. Thus, writing an entire paper for a student means that you may be undermining his or her entire future. Plenty of people do it, even so, but there is a better way.

You can still make some useful extra money helping students with term papers without writing the whole essay. Point them in the right direction in terms of research. Suggest organizational formats to them. Teach them how to use footnotes correctly and in a way that most fully displays the work they've done. Read their work before they turn it in and mark mistakes, as well as suggesting ways to improve their work. This approach is an exercise in tutoring rather than aiding and abetting plagiarism. You can feel good about what you are doing—teaching students how to put together an essay—and still make some extra money.

Greeting-Card Messages

When people appear to have more spending money than is consistent with their professional status, we tend to assume that they are good at playing the stock market or have some inherited income. But it may be that they are writing greeting-card messages. This is one of America's invisible secondary professions. The people who make extra money doing this work don't get credit, the way someone who writes articles in his or her spare time does, their work doesn't show up at craft shows, and they don't seem to be providing a visible service, but they are obviously up to something that pays for those exotic vacations or beautiful clothes!

Most greeting-card companies are happy to consider prose or verse messages, ranging from the sentimental to the funny, that are sent in by mail. They usually pay a flat fee for the work they accept, but when someone proves to be particularly good at this offbeat creative task, royalty arrangements can sometimes be worked out after a while. Some greeting-card companies are willing to accept a simple funny punch line together with a suggestion as to the front-of-card illustration that should accompany it, and they then assign an artist to do the drawing. The elite practitioners in this field provide both the drawing and the punch line.

If you have a gift for simple evocative verse—closer to advertising jingles than serious poetry—you may have a future in this invisible profession.

Children's Books

The mathematician Charles Dodgson, who lectured at Oxford University, made up stories to tell children, including the daughter of the dean of Christ Church, the Oxford college. The daughter's name was Alice Liddell, and it was for her that he originally created the story of *Alice's Adventures in Wonderland,* which he eventually published under the name the world knows him by, Lewis Carroll. And A. A. Milne originally made up the Winnie the Pooh stories for his son, whose name was indeed Christopher Robin.

In fact, the list of famous children's stories that were first created, quite casually, for a particular child could go on for pages. Do you tell made-up stories to your own children, as well as reading aloud to them? Have some of those stories seemed to strike a special chord with your kids and their friends? Then maybe you ought to be writing them down and sending them out to publishers. Although the market for adult novels, and many other books, has decreased in recent years, the sale of children's books is at an all-time high. Publishers are always on the lookout for good new ones, and they are the easiest kind of book to get a publisher to seriously consider without hiring an agent or having an established writing career.

If you are good at drawing, as well as making up children's stories, all to the good. Do your own drawings, and if the publisher likes them, too, you won't have to split your royalties with an artist. But publishers sometimes insist on picking their own artists. Don't get mad if that happens. Sign the contract for the text, and write another one.

Writing a Novel

Only a minority of the books published in the United States each year are written by full-time writers. The majority are written a page or two a day by people who have set aside the time, often getting up early before going off to full-time jobs. Many writers, it is true, have jobs that are related to words— teachers, journalists, or advertising people, for example. But a surprising number of successful writers, especially novelists, have "come out of nowhere," writing their first novel, or even their first several books, at the kitchen table.

One of the most famous of these has been Grace Metalious, the New England housewife who set the nation on its ear with the publication of her shocking first novel, *Peyton Place,* back in the 1950s. In more recent times, Danielle Steel, whose jet-set novels have become perennial best-sellers, wrote her first novel, *Passion's Promise*, at the kitchen table. That is also true of dozens of people who write mysteries and romance novels.

If you have a gift for writing, don't just dream about becoming a published author—sit down at the kitchen or dining room table and start telling a story. The easiest way to break into the ranks of published novelists is by writing a paperback romance novel. There is a voracious readership for these books, and the publishers need new writers all the time. Along with children's books, romance novels can get a first reading from a junior editor more easily than any other kind of book, so that an agent isn't necessary to get your first exciting contract.

Writing Articles for Newspapers and Magazines

Many people who don't have a gift for creating dialogue and fascinating plots, and wouldn't even consider writing a novel, make very good money in their spare time writing articles for magazines and newspapers. And in fact they have some advantages over those who want to be novelists. The majority of published articles are short, many only ten to twenty pages, which takes a lot less time to write than a 250-page novel. If a novel that has taken a writer two years to finish doesn't sell, it can be utterly discouraging. But the article writer is likely to have finished another one before the rejection slip comes in on the last one he or she wrote, and it's much easier to keep going until a sale is made. Rejection slips are a part of a writer's life, anyway. There is no writer who hasn't gotten one, and most have received many. An article can be rejected a dozen times and still go on to win a prize or be anthologized.

This is a very good time to be writing articles. There are dozens of "niche" magazines on the market, devoted to quite specialized areas of information or recreation. Do you know a lot about cigars, or macramé, or computers, or antiques? There's a magazine, usually several, that needs your expertise. Go to the library and ask to see *Writer's Market, Literary Marketplace*, or *The Writer's Yearbook*, which are usually kept at the main reference desk. They list hundreds of magazines that buy articles, briefly describing what they are looking for and whether you should query them about an idea first. And don't forget your local newspaper—that's how Erma Bombeck got her start.

Creating Crossword Puzzles

Are you one of those obnoxious people who do crossword puzzles in ink? Do the names of obscure South American rivers and cities in the steppes of Central Asia pop into your head at the slightest nudge? Then maybe you should be creating crossword puzzles instead of just doing them faster than everyone else. Almost every newspaper in the country, and many magazines, publish crossword puzzles, and most of them are put together by people working at home in their spare time. There's a great variation in the level of difficulty of published crossword puzzles, with *The New York Times Magazine* at the apex of complexity. You can start at a simple level and work your way up, although many people who work in this field are content to turn out quite simple puzzles year after year.

This is not a field that holds out the promise of potential fortunes, such as writing mysteries or romance novels, but it can bring in some nice extra money doing something you enjoy.

Grooming Pets

Yes, many veterinarians offer pet-grooming services. But many pets, especially dogs, hate to go to the vet, figure out what is about to happen ahead of time, and get the shakes or otherwise act up, making the owner feel guilty. For that reason, many dog and cat owners would prefer to take their pets someplace else for grooming. Some people have a real empathy with animals, knowing instinctively how to calm them down and make them behave. In fact, the person—usually a woman—who grooms pets for veterinarians always has that ability. They don't have veterinary degrees, and you don't have to have one either to go into the pet-grooming business.

This is a terrific extra-money sideline for people who love animals and have the knack for dealing with them.

Since it's a "by appointment only" business, you can keep good control of your time. Pet groomers can also do some secondary business in collars and leashes, fancy ribbons for those special dog and cat occasions, pet treats and toys. These can sell well—when a pet has just had a bath and a haircut and it is looking its best, owners are tempted to buy a new collar, and are very likely to want to reward the pet with a new toy for having gone through the grooming session without disgracing itself.

Dog and Cat Sitting

If you are good with animals, consider taking canine or feline guests into your home when people go on vacation. This is not a matter of running a kennel—only one pet at a time is taken for care, and it lives in the home with the "host" or "hostess." People will gladly pay you one hundred dollars a week to do this for them, since that's much cheaper than a good kennel and the pet's owner can feel more secure in the knowledge that his or her beloved dog or cat is not locked up in a cage and has individual, loving care.

Most people who do this kind of job simply stumbled into it, when asked by a friend to take care of a pet. It helps if you know the pet, especially if it's a dog, and in smaller communities that's often the case. Otherwise ask the owner to bring the pet over for a get-acquainted session before leaving town. This not only will help get the pet acclimated to you and your home, but can give you fair warning if the dog is clearly a neurotic, uncontrollable mess. In that case, make it clear that the animal's behavior is unacceptable and that you cannot take the responsibility of having it on hand. This will not lose you customers. If the owner complains to anyone who knows the dysfunctional pet, that person will simply think you're smart.

Always get partial payment in advance, and be sure that you have all the information needed about the animal's veterinarian. Many people who do this kind of work have commented that their animal guests are better behaved than the human variety.

Obedience School for Dogs

Ideally, as any dog book will tell you, a new puppy needs to have someone around all the time for it to be properly trained. But in this age of two-income households, that's seldom possible. And while some breeds of dog are fairly easy to train, and can be taught to behave even without the constant attention they ought to have, many others can turn out to be real problems. The dog that simply will not stop pulling on the leash, or that jumps up on everyone it sees (particularly if they're elderly or on crutches, it can seem), is going to need professional help.

If you have any background in dog training, or are simply very good with animals and willing to read a lot of books or take a course to give you a sense of authority, opening an obedience school for dogs in your backyard could pay real dividends. Be sure you have enough space to operate in (at least a quarter acre), and start small (unless you have solid experience), dealing with only one dog at a time. As your expertise increases, you may well be able to hold group classes, substantially increasing your income.

Some people who train dogs are willing to have the owner drop the dog off while they work alone with it for an hour. But most dog experts think it is much easier and more effective to have the dog's owner present. That's because in many cases the real problem isn't training the dog, but the owner. Some dog trainers find that an inoffensive way to make this clear to the owner is to say up front, "When the course is completed, your dog gets a rawhide treat, you get the diploma."

Togs for Dogs

In America, more money is spent on pet food than on any other consumable "need," even beer or breakfast cereals. We love our pets, and will do anything to keep them happy. Many short-haired and small dogs don't take to the cold very well. Dachshunds will start shivering on a cool night in August. The popularity of smaller dogs has been on the rise in recent years, and so has the sale of sweaters for them. Some people think sweaters for dogs are silly, but many owners believe they keep their dogs healthier. If someone is going to buy a sweater for a dog, he or she is going to want it to be a pretty one. That's where you expert knitters come in.

Sure, there are commercial dog sweaters for sale, but there's nothing like being able to boast that *your* pet's winter togs are handmade. And many people like the idea of having the pet's name emblazoned on the sweater, especially if it's an unusual name such as Zelda or Strudel. Yes, there are dog sweater patterns for sale from specialty companies, but if you're a good enough knitter to consider doing this professionally, you will no doubt be able to adapt a child's sweater pattern. All you need is the measurements. This is one case in which it can be worthwhile to spend the extra money for a small photo ad in the local paper. There's nothing like a picture of some adorable pup in one of your creations to bring the customers running. How much can you charge? Check out the prices of commercial dog sweaters in your area and add 50 percent.

Breed Pedigreed Puppies

This can be a costly endeavor at the beginning, but if you have the capital to get started, the breeding of pedigreed dogs can pay off handsomely in the long run, with the puppies selling for hundreds of dollars each. No one should get into this business who isn't willing to do a lot of hard work, but at the same time, it is the kind of work that can be very rewarding if you love animals.

Most dog books these days warn against buying "that puppy in the window" of the pet store, many of which come from "puppy mills," where they are carelessly bred and thus prone to hereditary diseases such as hip dysplasia (a congenital malformation that shows up when the dog becomes an adult). Even the august American Kennel Club has been accused of turning a blind eye to bad breeding practices. But for that very reason, people in the know are very careful about the dogs they buy. Once you have established yourself as a reputable small breeding operation—and it will take at least two or three years— you will find that customers will come from hundreds of miles away to purchase your puppies. The dog world is tightly knit, and a good reputation resonates far and wide.

If you think you have what it takes to do this kind of hard but rewarding and ultimately lucrative work, start by investigating your local and state laws regarding zoning, licensing, and health. Consult books, breeders (check the Internet), and show-dog owners, and work out a realistic three-year budget. If you then go forward, you may well find yourself with a lifelong interest that pays considerable dividends.

Telemarketing

This is the most common way for people to make extra money at home while working directly for another company. All you need is a telephone, a good clear voice—and a lot of patience. The patience is necessary because more people will say no to your pitch than yes, some will just hang up, and a few will abuse you. Everyone says they hate being interrupted with sales calls during the evening hours, but the business is here to stay because many of the same people do buy products, subscribe to magazines, or answer consumer polls when promised a free gift. Doing consumer polls is the most interesting work of this kind because the people you are calling quite often "get into" answering the questions and at least the semblance of a real conversation can take place.

Getting a telemarketing job usually involves some training sessions at a downtown location, but once you are hired, you can work entirely from your home, and in some cases the specific hours you work on a given night are up to you, provided you log a certain number of calls. Other situations are more regimented, and you will be required to make your calls during a specific time period because the company has found that it brings in the highest number of positive responses.

Some telemarketing jobs pay an hourly wage, others use a commission basis. Individuals who are good at this job can make substantial amounts of extra money. Such people are not only good at selling but have the capacity not to dwell on any negative experiences they have. It's not the easiest or most creative at-home job, but it can pay well.

Antique Dealing

Antiques can be sold in many ways. In major cities, many of the best antique dealers have showrooms that you would never even know were there from the street level, and see customers by appointment only. At the other extreme there are enormous sheds, such as the famous one in Adamstown, Pennsylvania, where hundreds of antique dealers display their wares in rooms, cubicles, or booths. But there are also a surprising number of people who sell antiques from their own homes. These tend to be in small cities, towns, and even rural areas where tourists are likely to be passing through to see the autumn leaves or on the way to some major historical site. An at-home antique dealership may be located in an old barn alongside the family residence. Or, on a smaller scale, some people sell antiques, particularly smaller pieces such as art glass, wind-up toys, dolls, pewter, or picture frames, from a room or two set aside at the front of the house for that purpose.

It's perfectly possible to bring in a considerable amount of extra money by opening such a display only on weekends, or five days a week in peak tourist season for the area. Many people who collect antiques particularly like to buy their treasures in this kind of location—it gives them a special pleasure to pick up a lovely piece in the quiet of a front parlor or the special light of an old barn instead of some vast arcade among hundreds of other customers. In fact, with the atmosphere of an at-home dealership working for you, it is often possible to get slightly higher prices for your antiques than you could elsewhere.

Rare Books

Most cities of any size have a rare- and used-book dealer—big cities will have many—but even the largest dealers regularly get requests for books that are out-of-print, or for rare signed first editions, which they do not have in stock. Such dealers will often tell a customer to give them a week and they will try to locate a copy. They don't want to call competitors, of course, even on the other side of the country, unless they absolutely have to. Instead, they have lists of private dealers and collectors—people who often work out of their own homes. If you love books and have experience in the field even as just a collector, you could certainly get into this fascinating and sometimes lucrative field.

Most people who deal in rare books from their homes specialize in certain kinds of books. That could mean first editions of novels or poetry, ornate limited editions, nineteenth-century children's books, books on natural history, the Civil War, or any of dozens of other special categories. Dealing in books of this kind can easily be a home-based venture, but it will, of course, be necessary to go out into the field to seek out books that are rare, difficult to find, or have been signed by the author. That means going to auctions of books as well as estate auctions where the contents of entire homes are sold. Even flea markets can sometimes yield an extraordinary find, selling for a few dollars yet worth a small fortune.

If you go into this field, write to large rare-book dealers across the country, letting them know your specialty.

These days, in addition, much buying and selling of rare books is starting to take place on the Internet.

Yard-Sale Broker

Yard sales are a great American pastime. In smaller cities, towns, and some suburban areas, there are numerous yard sales every weekend—and some people make the rounds of them on a very regular basis, as a form of entertainment. But many people who have plenty of things in their attics or cellars that they'd like to sell never seem to get around to it. They may not like the idea of dealing with strangers tramping around their yard, or think it's all too much work, or simply have no idea what prices to put on things. That's where you come in if you're somebody who gets a kick out of the whole yard-sale scene. Set yourself up as a broker, selling other people's things for them in your yard and taking a commission. Have your clients bring what they want to sell to your house in boxes. You will then take care of the pricing, and setting out the tables to display the goods for sale. Use a color-coded system of price stickers so you know exactly who brought each object to you. If you hold such sales every other weekend, at least, your sale will become a customary stop for people who are yard-sale fanatics. If you often have really good stuff, antique dealers are likely to show up as well—remember that the professionals will be waiting for you to set up as early as 7:00 A.M. This is no job for slugabeds.

Set a time limit with those who are supplying you with their yard-sale items, putting them out only for a couple of weekends. Since you are doing the main work, you should get at least a 40 percent commission, and some people who act as yard-sale brokers insist on a fifty-fifty split.

Taxidermy

Although the move toward heightened environmental awareness over the past several decades has resulted in shortened hunting seasons, greater restrictions on the amount of game that can be taken, and stiff penalties for out-of-season hunting, this traditional pastime of American sportsmen is still big business in states across the country. That means good business for anyone trained in taxidermy, or willing to learn the ancient trade. Because of the fairly brief hunting season these days, full-time taxidermists have become scarce. Most of those now operating do so on the side to earn extra money. And because they are much fewer in number than they once were, they can charge substantial prices for their exacting work.

Not every hunter wants a stuffed stag head on the wall in the den, or every fisherman a marlin mounted on the wall, but there are enough customers to make this a lucrative sideline. And once in a while you may get a really big job—remember that Roy Rogers had his famous movie horse Trigger stuffed.

Family Photos

Are you an expert photographer with your own darkroom? Put your expertise to work taking portraits of children and families, as well as resume photos. Yes, there are expensive studios in town that do this. But that's the problem, they're expensive. There are those very reasonable sets of ninety-nine photos offered at the mall. But in those everyone looks one step above a mug shot. If you know what you're doing, you can certainly beat the prices of a big studio with high overhead, and produce a more individual and better-looking portrait than the mall assembly lines.

You should have a den or family room with enough space to set up proper lighting, and some basic props and different-colored curtains or backgrounds to provide individuality. But you can also keep it simple and offer only black-and-white resume pictures. New photos are constantly needed by actors, writers, anyone who lectures frequently, and even, these days, by many businesspeople. Specializing in this kind of photography can bring you many referrals, since it is often harder to get good resume pictures taken than it is color family pictures.

Either way, offer your services by appointment only. Have a range of prices for different numbers and sizes of photo, and set your fees in between the "wedding studio" level and the mall variety.

VCR Tape Specials

Are you a whiz with your VCR? Do you have a large collection of videotapes? Do you have the standard equipment necessary to edit together snippets of various tapes? If so, you may have the makings of a specialty videotape service. I have a good friend who does this in his spare time. His Halloween tapes are hysterically funny, the Christmas tapes are uplifting, and what he has managed to do with old Bette Davis and Joan Crawford movies has to be seen to be believed. He doesn't sell these one-of-a-kind compilations in stores, he never uses more than a few minutes of any one movie or old television program, and he puts these snippets together in highly original ways. He is, admittedly, skirting the copyright laws, but the producing companies and law enforcement services more than have their hands full dealing with outright piracy of entire movies without trying to deal with this kind of personalized service.

And the service is personalized, depending entirely on word of mouth. Someone may want a birthday present for a spouse or friend who loves old musicals or dotes on 1950s horror movies. With a few hours work, my friend edits together an hour-long compilation of highlights, for which he charges twenty-five dollars. The charge is low because he has such a good time doing the job. And while he's not going to get rich with this sideline, it brings in money he can use to acquire—what else?—more tapes he wants for himself.

Games to Play

Back in the late 1970s, some young Canadian men sitting around having a good time realized that what they were really doing was playing a new game. They had the wit to recognize what they had and the discipline to work out a formal set of categories and rules that turned "goofing off" into major profits. The game they invented and marketed was called Trivial Pursuit. In an age of information overload and endless celebrity-watching, the game proved a natural and became the hottest seller in decades.

Although the major game manufacturers have staffs whose business it is to come up with new games, the ones that turn out to be most popular often come from supposed amateurs, including Monopoly and the Rubik's Cube. I've met a seventy-year-old accountant who has just sold a new form of three-dimensional chess, and a twenty-one-year-old computer whiz whose computer game will be on the market next year. It takes a special turn of mind to invent new games, but many people who come up with great ideas never pursue them properly, and then discover to their chagrin that someone else has had a similar idea and made a bundle from it.

If you are the kind of person who makes up games for your own entertainment, try developing one of your best ideas more rigorously. Try it out on friends and if the response is enthusiastic, it may be time to try selling it to a game manufacturer. Before you do, though, consult a lawyer about establishing your rights to your idea.

Bed-and-Breakfast

We are not talking about turning your Victorian house into a country inn here—that, at least during the tourist season, is a full-time job. A bed-and-breakfast situation, by contrast, can be handled even when both spouses have full-time jobs. People all over the country are making extra money this way. I know a couple in Texas who fixed up a one-room cottage on their property in the lovely hill country outside Austin. That required an initial investment of several thousand dollars, since they put in a new bathroom. But within two years they had a waiting list all year round. At one hundred dollars a night, their investment has repaid itself dozens of times over, bringing in an extra thirty thousand dollars a year.

At the start, this couple served coffee or tea and croissants for breakfast, which is the most usual offering. But they subsequently made an arrangement with a charming local restaurant, and gave their guests gift certificates covering the cost of breakfast. Some people in this business do serve more substantial breakfasts in their own homes, but that is not a crucial element in luring customers. An attractive setup in an area that has a lot of visitors is the only essential. Some people, rather than fixing up a separate little cottage, rent a room in their own home, although this works best in a large house with plenty of bathrooms.

Can the bed-and breakfast idea work if you have children? Absolutely. The Texas couple has three daughters, and all were under twelve when they began their side business. A final tip: it helps to have charm in this business, but leave your guests *alone*.

A Guest Room for the Elderly

As America has become more and more mobile, and its citizens have grown to live longer and longer, a great many elderly parents find themselves ending their days in nursing homes. But there are still many children who believe that their parents should have the comforts of home as long as possible, and have an elderly mother or father come live with them when they are no longer quite able to care for themselves but not really in need of the kind of medical care offered by a nursing home. Even so, there are times when the rest of the family needs to get away, or is taking a vacation that Grandma or Grandpa really wouldn't be up to. What to do? There are professionals who can be hired to come stay with the elderly patient, but this is almost as expensive as round-the-clock home nurses.

In many smaller cities and towns there is an alternative—a caring person or couple, often with some nursing or medical background, who take in Grandma or Grandpa for a weekend or a week. Such situations offer a guest room on the first floor, usually with a private bath and a television set. Meals are taken with the "hosts." If you have caretakers come to your home, one of the things you are paying for is the fact that they can't be at their own homes. Thus these guest rooms for the elderly, while not inexpensive, can still save quite a lot of money. And Grandma or Grandpa gets to feel as though he or she is having a little vacation, too.

If you have the right setup, and would be good at this kind of work, it can provide some extra income and a service that will bring you enormous gratitude from both your "guest" and his or her children.

House-Sitting

This is another kind of job for people who don't mind moving a lot. It is usually done by single people who like to keep their material possessions to a minimum. It is a good job for freelance writers and other independent sorts whose regular income is also earned at home.

There are always people looking for house-sitters. The owner may be a college professor on sabbatical, a corporate executive posted abroad for a year, or a retired couple making a trip around the world. They have very nice houses, often filled with valuable things, and they don't want to leave them unoccupied for a year, but they may not want to rent them, either, since that can bring on all kinds of problems. So they pay someone known to be extremely trustworthy to live in the house, look after the garden and any pets, take care of any emergency repairs (the owner's lawyer or bank is usually given the power to disburse funds for any emergency), and keep the house in top shape.

People often get into this kind of work by accident, when a friend asks them to do it, but then go on doing it for years. I know a woman who has been at it for a dozen years in a city with a population of only 135,000, never having to rent her own apartment in all that time.

FIVE

Home Business Success Stories

Nothing succeeds like success.
ALEXANDRE DUMAS, 1854

Throughout this book there have been references to the successes enjoyed by individuals who started at-home businesses in their spare time to make extra cash. Success in this kind of endeavor, as in anything else, involves skill, organization, hard work—and a little bit of luck doesn't hurt. Many people who start at-home businesses have known for some time that they have a talent they would like to put to better use. We all have multiple skills and several aspects to our lives, and it brings great satisfaction to make as much use as possible of all the talents we have at our disposal. It helps us to live more fully when we escape the pigeonholes that general opinion often likes to stuff us into. The fact that our main way of making a living tends to be seen as our identity doesn't mean that there isn't a lot more to us. A nurse may also have a real gift for flower arranging, a car salesman for painting portraits. It's worth keeping in mind that one of the greatest American poets of the twentieth century, Wallace Stevens, was also a high-level insurance executive throughout his working life, just as Charles Ives, the immensely influential composer, was. They were very good at business and made a great deal of money, but they will be best remembered for the extraordinary creative work that they did on the side.

In this final chapter, let's look more closely at some people who achieved success in their at-home spare-time businesses. With one exception, they are not household names. In most cases their at-home business has remained a spare-time pursuit, one that brings in extra cash and gives them other kinds of satisfactions as well. That is all they really wanted. Happy in their full-time jobs, they were just looking for a way to give them some additional cash to take vacations, buy a few luxuries, or help send their kids to college. There are people, of course, who do achieve national renown with efforts that began at the kitchen table or basement workroom. Already mentioned are writers such as Danielle Steel and Erma Bombeck. The Pepperidge Farm line of foods grew out of a home-kitchen bread-baking operation, and there are undoubtedly people right now concocting salsas or cookies who will one day see their products on supermarket shelves across the country. But not everyone has that kind of ambition, or wants the responsibility of expanding into a full-fledged multimillion-dollar enterprise. Success is something we have to measure for ourselves, and for a great many people it means a modest achievement, but one that gives them a fuller sense of having lived a life that capitalized on secondary as well as primary talents.

The Beachcombers

Doreen and Scott both had full-time jobs, he as a bank loan officer and she in real estate. Every summer they spent a month in Maine with their three school-aged sons. As a family they would collect seashells and driftwood on the windswept beaches, just for the fun of it. Then Doreen saw some driftwood art advertised in a mail-order catalog. She had taken some art courses at college, and her immediate reaction to the photographs in the catalog was, "I can do that." In fact, she thought she could do it better.

The family got serious about picking up driftwood in Maine that summer. Doreen spent the winter making sculptures, fitting together several pieces of driftwood in astonishing ways. After she had finished a few, she took them to a small gallery in the Boston suburb where they lived, and it agreed to show her work. Customers loved it. Part of the appeal was that everyone saw something different in any given sculpture, making them not only beautiful but wonderful conversation pieces.

Obviously, a single trip to Maine each year wasn't going to provide enough raw material. So the family would set out every other weekend, even in winter, driving up and down the Northeast coast in their van, looking for fresh supplies. Doreen laughs when she tells the story of how often she called out, "Stop the van." The children got to the point where they started calling her, in good humor, "Stop the Van" instead of "Mama." She recalls the night she heard her youngest, Keith, saying his prayer.

"God bless Daddy," he concluded, "Tim, Scotty, me, Keith, and most of all Stop the Van."

"I've never laughed so hard in my life," Doreen says.

As the years went by, Doreen's driftwood sculptures started appearing in many corporate office buildings in the Boston area. She now mounts them on marble bases, and the larger ones sell for as much as three thousand dollars. Keith is in college now, and so is Scotty; Tim has already graduated. But Doreen and Scott still drive up and down the coast looking for driftwood, and the boys come along when they're home. There's no stopping "Stop the Van."

The Frozen Pumpkin

Just to show that there are many ways to practice a similar kind of work, consider the story of Pat Mayes. She, too, makes sculptures, and mounts them, but they're much smaller. And although, like Doreen, she stumbled into her extra-money profession, she didn't even have to leave the house to do it.

Pat Mayes works in department-store window display, and has a lot of artistic talent, but she had no idea she was about to embark on a new sideline when she carved her usual Halloween pumpkin a decade ago. This nice fat pumpkin had a terrifically ghoulish face and it held up longer than pumpkins usually do, so that she kept it almost until Thanksgiving. She noticed that it was beginning to sag one evening when guests were about to arrive for dinner, and hurriedly set it on the fire escape outside her top-floor apartment. And then she completely forgot about it.

It wasn't until spring, after a very snowy winter, that

she found the pumpkin again. Something strange and wonderful had happened to it in the course of the winter. It had collapsed even further, but the result was surprisingly beautiful in a weird way. Instead of throwing it away at long last, she decided to dry it in a very slow oven to see what would happen. It kept its shape, and after airing it further on the fire escape, she polyurethaned it, giving it several coats. Then she hot-glued it to a Lucite base. "It was so ugly it was fabulous," she says. "Scared me to death." She took it in to show her co-workers, who thought it was wonderful. "It looked like Quasimodo on a bad day," Pat remembers, "but that's just why people liked it. And it *was* unique."

That year Pat moved to a house with a small backyard. She built a wooden platform out back, and that Halloween she carved about twenty-five pumpkins with a variety of faces. That year she deliberately left them out back on the platform all winter. Her plan was to give a number of them to her friends and co-workers the following spring. But in the course of the winter, a new boutique opened in her neighborhood, and on a lark she took in the one mounted pumpkin she had and asked if they would be willing to try to sell it for her. They said yes, and even placed it in the window. "I happily went on with my errands, and on my way back home, when I looked in the window, my pumpkin was gone. I thought, well, they decided that was a little too adventuresome, but I went in anyway, and the lady who owned the shop smiled and gave me thirty dollars for my 'thing.' Remember, this was the dead of winter, halfway between Halloweens. The thirty dollars more than paid for the groceries I'd bought, and I had the feeling I wouldn't be giving away many of the frozen pumpkins I had sitting in my backyard after all."

Starting the next fall, Pat made trips to the country as soon as the pumpkin harvest was in and bought a couple of hundred of them. She spent weeks carving them, and enlarged her backyard platform to hold them. She eventually started placing electric lights in them to increase their impact, and now sells a thousand a year at fifty to one hundred dollars each. People buy them year-round at the several stores that carry them across the state, yet her work is seasonal, involving the carving of them in the fall and the preparing and mounting of them in the spring. "Now, this is what I call a moonlighting job," she says. "Not only do pumpkins grow at night, but I'm constantly taking a peek into the backyard on moonlit winter nights, seeing all that snow-covered money sitting there waiting for spring."

Beer-Can Planes

Doug spent his working life as a welder. He was devoted to his wife, Bessie, and shattered when she died of cancer at the age of fifty-eight. "It hit me awfully hard," he says. "To tell you the truth, I took to drink. Not the hard stuff and not during the day, it didn't get that bad, but I was drinking an awful lot of beer. And I got sloppy about the housekeeping. Really, Bessie had done that. So the beer cans would pile up and I'd put them in a sack the day before garbage pickup. But one day when I was cleaning up, I thought, Hey, I could have some fun with these. So I got out my metal shears and started cutting away. Made me an airplane!"

He liked what he saw and made some more, experimenting with different designs. His favorite was a bi-plane, with one wing on top of another, like the old beauties you see at air shows. He worked out a way to attach a propeller that moved, and went to a craft store and bought miniature rubber wheels. A piece of plastic wire mounted at the center of the wing made it possible to hang them, and when a small breeze came up, the propeller would actually turn. "I thought they were really cute," he says, "but they were just something to occupy my time."

Although he and Bessie hadn't had any children, he did have some grandnephews and nieces, and he gave them some, and passed out a number to kids in his neighborhood. The kids loved them. "What surprised me," he says, "was that grown-ups liked them a lot, too. I guess we all have some kid left in us." People told him he should sell them. So he made up about a hundred and rented a space at a flea market. The planes were small, only about five inches from wing tip to wing tip, but that first day he sold every single one at five dollars apiece. By chance, a Budweiser distributor saw his planes and asked if he could make about three hundred of them for the company Christmas tree. Doug thought that was a nice way to make an extra fifteen hundred dollars.

"That was years ago," Doug says. "But it sure started something." Now seventy-one, Doug still makes his airplanes, but he also creates animals, flowers, and even miniature houses. "With my pension, Social Security, and my aluminum cans, I have a very nice life. Went on a cruise last winter and met a very nice lady in her sixties. She lives down South. We'll see." Doug uses soft-drink cans as well as beer cans these days. He pays kids to collect the soft-drink cans, and friends bring him all their empty beer cans. "I hardly ever have a beer anymore myself," he says with a wink. "Too busy."

The Last Laugh

"I was the most hated man in town," says Herb. "According to the experts and all the rules, I did my job well. But on several occasions I had kids throw rotten eggs or fruit at me. And Halloween was always a nightmare. All the trees around my house would end up festooned with toilet paper. Ever try to get that out of trees? If it rains, you're in real trouble."

How did this man bring down the wrath of the kids in his Texas town on him? Was he the dogcatcher? A truant officer? No, he was the head dietician for the public school system. "The food was nutritious, and it was well prepared. I ate it myself every day. But it wasn't what the kids wanted. For one thing, it was never fried, and even worse, there was always a vegetable. They saw me as the embodiment of the worst side of their parents. 'It's good for you' is not their idea of a motto to live by."

But in truth, Herb had some better ideas about food himself. Such good ideas, in fact, that he won a number of local cooking contests, then moved on to the state level. That brought him some publicity, and got some of his recipes published in newspapers. The local paper finally asked him to do a food column in the late 1970s, when the interest in cooking news was growing all across the country. But he made a smart decision and used a fictitious name. "I could hear the jokes coming a mile away," he said. Eventually he put together a cookbook of regional recipes—including a lot of fried foods—and published it himself in a spiral-bound edition. "The big cookbook publishers in New York pay no attention," he says, "but people *like* inexpensive spiral-bound cookbooks. Over the years I've met dozens of people who've published their own little cookbooks, and they sell very well. I've sold sixty thousand copies of my latest in a year, at $14.95 each. My profit was four dollars a book. That's almost a quarter of a million dollars."

Needless to say, Herb no longer works for the school system. The kids aren't eating his nutritious menus at lunch. But they are eating his food at home. A lot of their mothers prepare dinners from Herb's cookbooks.

A Christmas Bonus

Laura G. started making Christmas ornaments when she was in her mid-twenties and pregnant for the first time. She and her husband didn't have much money, but they had a lot of friends. Using the pinecones that lay under trees all over town in the late fall, Laura created striking ornaments by painting the cones in different colors, following the natural line of the cones' spiral growth. "I still have a dozen of them," she says, "and they've aged well—just like me."

Her friends were thrilled with the cones. "Louise, my oldest friend, said, 'Honey, you should stop giving these beautiful things away and market them.' I just laughed." But then, shortly after the birth of her daughter, Laura's car was rear-ended by a drunken driver, and she was left paralyzed from the waist down. "I was a mess for a while," she says. "But I had my beautiful baby, and my husband was absolutely wonderful to me. I began to realize that I was luckier than a lot of people, and I pulled myself together. David was given the first of many promotions, but we had a lot of expenses because of my situation, so I decided to see what would happen if I took Louise's advice and tried to sell my Christmas ornaments. After all, it was something you did sitting down anyway."

Laura started small, making only about four hundred ornaments the first year, which she sold through a local gift shop. As time went on, she developed many new varieties of ornaments, and became more and more proficient. "I've been in this wheelchair seven years," she says, "but every year my business has grown. I have a wonderful family, and David is doing so well that I really wouldn't have to sell my Christmas ornaments if I didn't want to. But they've become part of my life. It's a lot of work, but it makes me happy. There are a lot of things I can't do, but this is something I'm good at that most people aren't."

Laura now has two employees helping her part-time. There have been suggestions of starting a full-fledged company and going national, but Laura prefers things as they are. "It's just right for me as it is," she says. "I think of it as a Christmas bonus." In fact, it's quite a bonus. She now sells four thousand ornaments a year, and the price has gone from the original five to fourteen dollars per ornament.

The Pie Lady

Laura, Herb, and the others whose stories have already been told have been written up in local newspapers. But Deborah Tyler, whose customers call her the Pie Lady, was given a lengthy article in *The New York Times* in the summer of 1997. Reporter Judith Zimmer wrote, "It's not much different from any other home in Nyack, N.Y., except for all the drivers who pull up and then leave with little white boxes. And there's that wonderful aroma and the wooden sign in the backyard that says, HOMEMADE PIES."

Ms. Tyler, the *Times* notes, learned to make pastry when she attended college in England and worked in the school kitchen. There she discovered that you have to take command when dealing with pie dough, and not let it talk back. "Everyone I knew who made pies and every cookbook make it sound so mysterious. 'If you do this, that will go wrong.' " Like so many at-home workers, Ms. Tyler got the idea for selling pies from an article she read about another woman who was doing it in Maine. Her response was to utter that all-important sentence: "If she can do it, why can't I?"

Ms. Tyler also knew instinctively to take a step that has been recommended in this book. She gave her first pies away to create word of mouth. This worked so well for her that she has never advertised—aside from that wooden sign outside her house, of course. Working in a "converted bedroom next to the family kitchen," she bakes as many as twenty-five pies a day toward the weekend, but sometimes as few as five, and is closed on Mondays. Almost all her pies are baked to order for people who have telephoned ahead. She is leery of expansion, although many people have urged it. "There's always this question in my mind," she told the *Times*. "At what point does a pie stop being homemade? I want to keep that back-door feeling wherever I go."

Traffic-Stopping Nail Polish

Her name is Dineh Mohajer, and she became the founder of a nationally known company at the age of twenty-one. That was not the result of a grand plan. She had been making batches of nail polish at home for herself and her friends for several months when she began her own company out of her home. She had been doing a lot of hard research work for her premed degree and needed a break. "Nail polish is pretty easy to whip up," she blithely told *Bottom Line* magazine in February 1997. But what Dineh was "whipping up" in the summer of 1995 was not just ordinary nail polish. The colors were extraordinary, very bright and intense.

Her boyfriend went around to a boutique in Santa Monica, where a friend worked, and the shop agreed to carry Dineh's line. "Within a few weeks, two well-known movie actresses wore my sky blue nail polish on the 'Late Show with David Letterman,' and MTV did a piece on us for its 'House of Style' fashion show." And so Dineh found herself taking a leave from college and searching for someone to serve as the chief executive officer of her fast-growing company, which she had given the wonderful name Hard Candy. She'd already moved her business out of the house into a small office, but still couldn't keep up with a 25 percent–a–month growth rate. With real business expertise in place, the company went from producing 450 bottles a month to 75,000.

Dineh notes that it wasn't her business skills that made Hard Candy successful. "It became successful because my boyfriend and I created nail polish that people liked." But they also were smart enough to know when they needed business help and hired top-notch people fast. There's a lesson in that for anyone whose home business suddenly takes off. You never know when huge success will strike out of the blue—sky blue in Dineh's case—but if that happens, you need to be ready to bring in professional businesspeople who can handle that kind of incredible growth.

Personalized Success

Almost everyone has seen a Lillian Vernon catalog, and millions of people have placed orders with this mail-order company, founded by Lillian Katz. That's because she scours the globe for handsome gifts and household items that are that rare combination of good quality and low price. I once bought a set of nesting baskets from her company that everyone admired, and which they invariably thought must have cost $50 or more. The real price: $14.95.

The company now processes more than five million orders a year, but it began in 1951 when Lillian was a pregnant housewife in Mount Vernon, New York. She had an idea. She would sell handbags and belts from her home, by mail, offering free personalizing for each piece. People like having their monograms on things, and the small operation had a quick success. A small initial ad in *Seventeen* brought in more than thirty thousand dollars in orders. Within a few years she moved the business out of her home, and now has not only corporate headquarters in New Rochelle, New York—not far from her starting place—but a distribution complex in Virginia Beach, Virginia, that is the last word in contemporary, computerized efficiency.

Even as the company grew into a national concern, Lillian Katz drew on the help of her two sons, who went from packing cartons as teenagers to becoming officers of the company. She has said that if you can run a home well, you can also run a small business well. But she also knew how to run a big business well. Not everyone has that kind of drive and organizational ability, and many will be perfectly happy to have their small business stay that way. And if unexpected big success comes, as it did to Dineh Mohajer and Hard Candy, most people are likely to need professional business help.

Every day, men and women across the country are starting home-based small businesses just to earn some extra cash—and often to draw on talents that haven't been fully explored or used. They're not looking too far down the line, or expecting to become millionaires, but sometimes that does happen. For hundreds of thousands of other people, success is measured on a smaller scale in terms of monetary gain, but the success quotient is often just as large in terms of personal satisfaction as it is for someone like Lillian Katz.